12|2

MOMMA CHERRI'S SOUL IN A BOWL COOKBOOK

CHARITA JONES

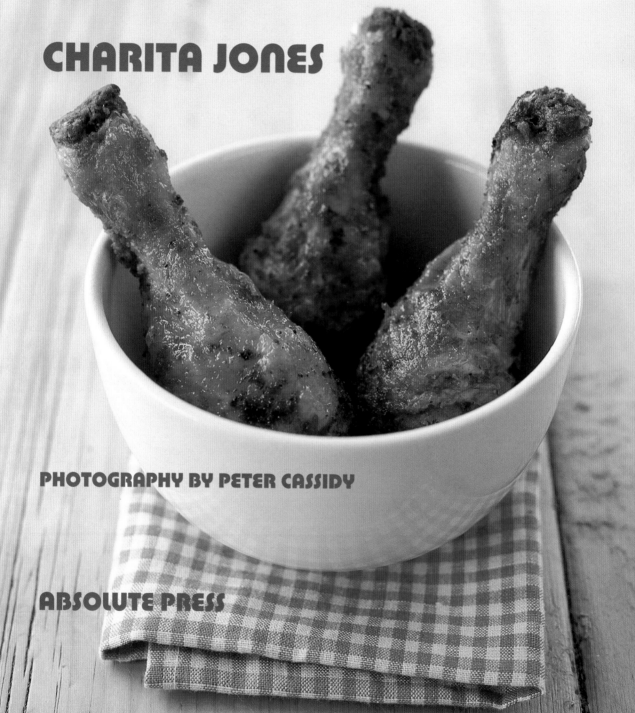

PHOTOGRAPHY BY PETER CASSIDY

ABSOLUTE PRESS

This book is dedicated to my wonderful nephew, Daood, and to my daughter's best friend, Faye. Both enjoyed life, happiness and soul food.

They will be especially remembered at each Thanksgiving, when we all give thanks and remember our departed loved ones in our hearts and souls.

First published in Great Britain
in 2007 by

Absolute Press
Scarborough House
29 James Street West
Bath BA1 2BT
Phone 44 (0) 1225 316013
Fax 44 (0) 1225 445836
E-mail info@absolutepress.co.uk
Website www.absolutepress.co.uk

Photography copyright
© Peter Cassidy

All photography Peter Cassidy, except pages 7
and 11, courtesy of the author.

Publisher Jon Croft
Commissioning Editor Meg Avent
Designer Matt Inwood
Publishing Assistant Meg Devenish

Editor Jane Middleton
Photographer Peter Cassidy
Props Stylist Cynthia Inions
Food Stylist Charita Jones

www.soulinabowl.com

A catalogue record of this book is available from
the British Library

ISBN 13: 9781904573593

Printed and bound by Butler & Tanner, Frome,
Somerset, England

A note about the text
This book was set using Helvetica Neue and Pump.
Helvetica was designed in 1957 by Max Miedinger
of the Swiss-based Haas foundry. In the early
1980s, Linotype redrew the entire Helvetica family.
The result was Helvetica Neue. Pump was designed
in 1970 by the Letraset Type Studio, echoing the
simple, geometric, sans-serif Bauhaus style so
popular from earlier in the century.

CONTENTS

SO YOU WANNA KNOW WHAT SOUL FOOD IS?

SOUL FOOD COMES FROM WITHIN.

It is a style of cooking that developed in the American Deep South when black people were enslaved, before the Civil War and the beginnings of emancipation. Expected to survive on leftover scraps of food, they just got on with cooking up some of the tastiest meals imaginable, in giant seasoned cast-iron pots.

Traditionally slave rations consisted of corn, bacon or salt pork, molasses, flour and seasonal fruits and vegetables. With these few items, they managed to create a surprising variety of wholesome dishes. They learned how to use everything – nothing was wasted or taken for granted. If the master and his family ate a leg of pork, the slaves enjoyed the leftover bits, such as succulent pig's feet, the ears, tail, head and the delicious intestines, commonly known as chitterlings. Stale bread was turned into stuffings or puddings, damaged or overripe fruit used in drinks or desserts, leftover vegetables made into croquettes or hush puppies.

In the 1960s, following the abolition of segregation, the Black Consciousness movement sprang up. Black artists were noted for their soulful blues music and the word 'soul' became popular: soul man, soul music and, of course, soul food. This became the common term used to describe the African-American style of cooking that had evolved from the days of slavery. Soul food quickly grew in popularity and by the late 1960s soul food restaurants were opening up all over America. Although the cooking style originated in the Deep South, now every city with a large black population – Chicago, New York, Los Angeles, Washington DC – has a thriving soul food culture.

Sunday dinner is an important soul food occasion. It is the time when the family gathers together after church to prepare a large meal. Often it is a potluck affair, where various family members each contribute a dish or two to the table. Traditional dishes might include Southern-fried chicken, fried catfish, cornbread, jambalaya, candied sweet potatoes, Hoppin' John and delicious barbecue ribs. You will find recipes for all of these in this book.

Since the Civil Rights movement in the 1950s and 1960s, Europeans have taken a great interest in Black American culture. The UK in particular has a tradition of opening its doors to a host of different cultures and influences, especially in music, fashion and food. There has always been a closeness between the British and the Americans – they are almost like cousins – but now the family has widened and British youth has embraced the Black hip hop scene. If you trace this and other popular music back to its roots, you end up with soul music – which brings us back to soul food.

The first American restaurant in Europe was, in fact, a soul food restaurant, called Haynes. It opened in Paris in the 1940s and became a popular spot for American artists of all kinds. It was a familiar place to meet up with other ex-patriots and, most importantly, to sample good, home-cooked food. Haynes is still going strong. I visited it in 2003 and it was great to discover that soul food is soul food worldwide.

Little Charita on her Daddy's knee, 1957.

SO YOU WANNA KNOW WHAT SOUL FOOD IS?

THE BIRTH OF MOMMA CHERRI'S

I CAME TO LONDON IN 1978
WITH AN AMERICAN TOURING THEATRE COMPANY, WHICH OPENED IN THE WEST END WITH A GOSPEL MUSICAL.

The show didn't last long but I knew London was for me. I had always felt something of a misfit before but in London I discovered that I could express myself. Both my daughters, Katryna and Krystin, were born in the UK, I have two grandchildren, Ellis and Tyler, and in the past I have fostered more than 40 children and teenagers. So cooking big family meals is a way of life for me.

In 2000, after getting remarried, I decided with my husband, Phil, to relocate to Brighton and open the UK's only soul food restaurant. It was a big step for both of us. I had lived in London for 22 years and Phil was from Manchester. Momma Cherri's Soul Food Shack opened its doors to the public in 2001, the name Cherri being my childhood nickname (no one could ever pronounce Charita). We tried to give the restaurant the feel of being in someone's front room – I wanted it to seem as if I was welcoming people into my home. There were framed original Ebony magazine covers from the 1960s and 1970s decorating the walls, along with the American flag, pictures of Martin Luther King Jr, family photos, a shelf packed with soul food cookbooks, black history books, homemade placemats filled with family photos, black history facts, and soul music and trivia quizzes on the tables. We have always had a loyal local following and each weekend Brighton fills up with tourists, who flock to us to discover the secrets of genuine soul food.

Although we were popular from the start, we simply didn't have enough customers throughout the week to enable us to pay our bills. I knew the food inside out but my husband and I struggled with the business side of things. By 2004 we had run out of money and needed professional help.

Left: Momma Cherri's Soul Food Shack... where it all began
Below: Momma Cherri's Big House

KITCHEN NIGHTMARES!

CLOSE TO CLOSURE, AND DESPERATE TO SAVE THE BUSINESS,
I DECIDED TO TAKE A GAMBLE
AND VOLUNTEERED TO APPEAR ON TELEVISION'S *KITCHEN NIGHTMARES* SERIES.

Legendary chef, Gordon Ramsay, and his team arrived in December 2004 and immediately set about making changes to our management style. Gordon also helped us rationalise the menu, suggesting a tapas-style deal, which we christened Soul in a Bowl, hence the title of this book. I'm proud to say that the big difference between Momma Cherri's and the other places featured on the programme was that Gordon loved our food. In fact, he said it was the first time he had cleaned his plate during the whole series. We got on great, and I have since built on all his wise suggestions. He took me out of the kitchen and encouraged me to mingle with my customers, helping them to understand what soul food is all about.

It goes without saying that Gordon Ramsay's intervention was our salvation. The programme first aired in June 2005 and has since been shown across the world, putting us on the international food map. Previously we had been serving about 150 meals a week. After the programme was first shown, this increased to 1,000 a week, and we were having to turn away over 80 people a day. We went from having no business to being in a position where we couldn't fit everyone in. There was an immediate interest in soul food, culture and music and, to my amazement, in me, I was invited to appear regularly on national television, in shows such as 'Saturday Kitchen' and 'Great Food Live'. Eventually, to accommodate the demand, we closed the original Soul Food Shack and moved to much larger premises, Momma Cherri's Big House. It's been an uphill journey, with triple the staff, triple the bills, triple the covers, triple the food and drink, but one hundred times the fun and excitement.

So, it finally happened. After all those years of hard work and great food, all of us here at Momma Cherri's got the break we needed. Thanks to Gordon Ramsay and the *Kitchen Nightmares* team, we're now one of the top foodie attractions in Brighton. Wow! Who would have thought it, considering how close we were to closing?

Gordon with Charita on his visit to the restaurant

HOW TO USE THIS BOOK

WHEN I BEGAN WRITING THIS BOOK,
I THOUGHT IT WOULD BE A QUICK AND EASY TASK. AFTER ALL, I HAVE BEEN COOKING FOR MOST OF MY LIFE, AND THE SOUL FOOD COOKING STYLE IS NATURAL TO ME.

It has been pumping through my veins and fuelling my soul for more than a half a century. But I ran into unexpected problems when it came to converting American weights and measures to British ones. I had never used a set of scales to weigh anything before – in the States we measure everything in cups. Besides, I am a 'pinch-dash-sprinkle-handful' type of girl. Shucks, where I grew up we just chose a cup to use and stuck to it. Somehow, the recipes worked out.

Now just because I said I had trouble adapting to the British system doesn't mean I didn't get it right in the end. This book has been written with you, the British, in mind. It has been carefully edited and the recipes have been independently tested to make sure they are right. I want you to feel safe that what I have written is completely reliable. Having said that, I like to think that you will use the recipes as a guide only. Don't feel you need to stick to the exact letter of them. Soul food cooking should be a personal journey and you should feel free, just like my enslaved forefathers, to explore and experiment, adding your own personal touch to the dishes.

I am of the belief that if you season your pot, you can't go wrong. Let me explain. I look at the size of the pot and evenly sprinkle the seasoning across the top – the bigger the pot, the more you need. Let's face it, if you were cooking for four, you wouldn't use a huge pot, you'd use a small to medium one, so you will be able to judge and get it right. I also season at the beginning of a recipe, when the onions, peppers, etc. go in.

Remember, you can always add more spices and flavourings to your dishes but it's very difficult to take them away, so go easy at first with the salt, pepper, Cajun seasoning and chilli. Taste and add more if you need to, add additional flavours if you think the dish can take it, but most of all enjoy what you cook, and make each dish your own.

I should also point out that I have never been able to cook a meal designed for just two people, so all of the recipes will feed more. I believe that whenever you cook you should be aware that someone might knock on your door, and there should always be enough in your pot to share. The essence of soul food is sharing what you have. And let's face it, if you make a dish that the family likes, you want to be able to offer seconds, or at least to know that there is some left over for lunch the next day, or even to freeze for another occasion.

MANY OF THE DISHES I COOK ARE CREATED AFTER I'VE CHECKED WHAT'S AVAILABLE IN THE CUPBOARD OR AFTER I'VE BEEN SHOPPING.

One of my favourite days is market day. In Brighton we have a Sunday market at the train station, where you can acquire all sorts of bargains. Most towns now have regular markets, including farmers' markets. These are great because not only do you support local producers if you shop there, but you can also trace the food back to its source. This way of shopping goes right back to my roots. Slaves had to grow their own food, or go to open markets to buy or trade goods. As money was always tight, looking for a bargain was a way of life.

I was brought up not to waste anything and to use my initiative and imagination when shopping and cooking. I buy whatever looks good, particularly if it's on special offer, then decide what I'm going to cook. Don't be afraid to ask what the vendor has 'left over' or close to its sell-by date. Just because something is going cheap doesn't necessarily mean it's inferior. Many vendors throw away a lot of vegetables and fruit at the end of the day because they are bruised or overripe – often all they need is a sharp knife to cut away the bad bits and you will be amazed how much goodness is left. Don't be afraid to ask for a deal or to point out imperfections in your 'soon to become' purchases. Believe it or not, stallholders still like to engage in cheerful banter and often welcome a chat with customers.

A good time to shop is after a holiday, when there is an abundance of seasonal fruit and vegetables. A typical haul for me on a Sunday would include a nice piece of local meat, potatoes, apples, pears, butternut squash, pumpkins, cucumbers, onions, melons, plus overripe tomatoes, avocados and plums. With all of this, I cook a full Sunday roast and a dessert, and have loads left over to make sauces, stews and unusual dishes.

Finally, a word about the Soul in a Bowl website. You can order a few of the things you'll find in these recipes online. My Cajun spice seasoning, for example – mild, medium or hot! – and other soul food condiments such as gumbo file and corn bread. You can even order yourself a Momma T-Shirt or apron! There are discounts available to use against following orders or restaurant bookings. Check it out and let's spread some virtual soul!

www.soulinabowl.com

SOUL IN A BOWL

SOUL IN A BOWL IS TO SOUL FOOD WHAT TAPAS AND DIM SUM ARE TO SPANISH AND CHINESE FOOD: BITE-SIZED SAMPLE DISHES FROM THE MAIN MENU.

We set it up after Gordon Ramsay suggested that we offer a selection of soul dishes in small bowls on a tray for people to share. He felt the customers didn't know enough about soul food to make the right choices, and were nervous about ordering dishes they'd never heard of. Soul in a Bowl would educate their palates, so on their next visit they could tackle the main menu with more confidence. In fact, this hasn't really happened.

SOUL IN A BOWL IS SO POPULAR, AND SUCH GOOD VALUE, THAT THE MAJORITY OF RETURN CUSTOMERS STICK TO IT.

A TYPICAL SOUL IN A BOWL TRAY:

Fried Catfish Goujons
Hot Buffalo Chicken Wings
Southern-Fried Chicken
BBQ Ribs
Momma's Meat Jambalaya
Macaroni and Cheese

Succotash
Cornbread
Sweet Potato Salad
Coleslaw
A mixed salad

SOUL IN A BOWL IS A GREAT WAY TO GET A PARTY STARTED AT HOME. I HAVE PUT TOGETHER A FEW SUGGESTIONS TO SUIT YOUR VARIOUS PARTY NEEDS:

A BREAKFAST OR BRUNCH PARTY

American Pancakes
French Toast
Bacon
Fried Apples

Hash Browns
Corned Beef Hash with Poached
 Eggs and Salsa

A DINNER PARTY

Nachos with Tomato Salsa and
 Guacamole
Hot Buffalo Chicken Wings
Fried Catfish Goujons
Rev. Daisy's Southern-Fried Chicken
Momma's Meat Jambalaya
Vegetable Jambalaya

Brother Brian's BBQ Ribs
Meatballs
Corn Salad with Black-eyed Peas
Devilled Eggs
Coleslaw
Key Lime Pie
Pineapple Upside-Down Cake

A THANKSGIVING OR CHRISTMAS DINNER

Roast Turkey and Cornbread Stuffing
Cranberry Sauce
Pig's Trotters
Brother Brian's BBQ Ribs
Cajun Potato Wedges
Candied Sweet Potatoes

Spring Greens and Kale with Ham
 Hocks
Cornbread
Hoppin' John
Roast Vegetable Trio
Sweet Potato Pie with Pecans
Peach Cobbler

A CHILDREN'S PARTY

Nachos (fried tortilla strips) with
 Tomato Salsa and Guacamole
Fried Catfish Goujons
Buffalo Chicken Wings
 (without the hot sauce)

Southern-Fried Chicken Nuggets
Mini Homemade Burgers
Macaroni and Cheese
Cajun Potato Wedges
Chocolate Brownies

Clockwise from bottom-left Southern-fried Chicken, Momma's Meat Jambalaya, Sweet Potato Salad

Clockwise from bottom-left Momma's Soulatouille, Roast Curried Pumpkin, Fried Jerk Red Snapper

Clockwise from bottom-left Momma's Spicy Fishcakes, BBQ Ribs, Catfish Goujons

Clockwise from bottom-left Soul Breakfast with cornbread, hash browns, fried apples, fried eggs and crispy bacon, Blueberry Pancakes, Cornbeef Hash with Poached Egg and Homemade Tomato Salsa

17

BREAKFAST

AMERICAN-STYLE PANCAKES

MOMMA'S REAL AMERICAN BREAKFAST

COUNTRY OMELETTE
CORNED BEEF HASH
WITH POACHED EGGS AND SALSA
TROPICAL FRUIT SMOOTHIE

AMERICAN-STYLE PANCAKES

Now to tell the truth, you haven't really had an American breakfast if you haven't had a round of pancakes and what we call French toast (page 22). These aren't your thin, European-style crêpes with lemon and sugar. No, these are plump, light, fluffy pancakes. These are the real deal.

Believe it or not, some of the best pancakes come straight from a box. There are many good-quality American brands, which sell all over the world. I use them regularly but if you can't find them and want to make pancakes from scratch, here's a quick and easy way to do it. I must admit, since making my own, I love pancakes even more!

MAKES 10–12

300g plain flour
2 teaspoons baking powder
100g caster sugar
2 eggs
250ml milk
90g butter, melted, plus extra to serve
maple syrup, to serve

Optional goodies (about 50g of any of the following): fresh fruit, chocolate chips, bacon, drippings

We're gonna try and make light, fluffy pancakes, and this requires sifting the flour and baking powder into a bowl and then stirring in the sugar. Using a hand whisk, mix the eggs and milk together, then slowly add them to the dry ingredients, mixing until you have a smooth batter. It should be thicker than a traditional British pancake batter but still loose enough to pour. Let it stand for at least 5 minutes, then add half the melted butter, plus whatever else you like – blueberries, sliced strawberries, diced peaches and chocolate chips are all great favourites. If you are using bacon, cut it up and fry it in a pan, then add the bacon and 1–2 tablespoons of its fat to the batter at the last minute for a nice savoury flavour.

To cook the pancakes, pre-heat a large, flat, non-stick (preferably cast iron) frying pan and add enough of the remaining butter to cover the base. If you have just fried bacon, pour off any excess fat, if necessary, and use the same pan. The pan needs to be really hot in order for the pancakes to cook properly, but be careful not to burn the butter. Using a small ladle or jug, pour enough batter into the hot pan to form a circle about the size of a small saucer – you should be able to fit in 2 or 3 at a time. Cook for about 1 minute on each side, until golden brown and slightly risen. The first pancake you cook will always be a mess, that's just the way it is, but the lesson is, you'll then know if you need to turn up the heat or reduce it. So the first, like most things in life, is just a trial. It's a good thing. Once you get to the third, they'll be perfect.

As the pancakes are done, turn them out and stack them up with a knob of butter between each one. You can keep them warm in a low oven, covered with a piece of foil. Serve with butter and maple syrup – plus, if you like, fried eggs, Hash Browns (page 24), Bacon (page 22) and/or sausages.

MOMMA'S REAL AMERICAN BREAKFAST

When I arrived in England I was very impressed with the traditional English breakfast. It reminded me of a good American breakfast without the pancakes and French toast. I soon realized that whenever I was real hungry I would hunt out a nice greasy spoon for an all-day breakfast! I've since learnt that the American breakfast was derived from the full English breakfast but featured mostly sweet or mild-flavoured foods. For me, breakfast is *the* meal of the day. I like to cook and serve it morning, noon, and often as a hearty supper time treat.

FRENCH TOAST

This is sweet, moist, gently fried bread that you stack up and smother in butter and maple syrup. Many people confuse it with 'eggy bread' but it's more than that. The sugar, vanilla and cinnamon turn it into a delightful sweet treat.

FOR 2

3 eggs
100ml milk
2 tablespoons caster sugar
1/4 teaspoon ground cinnamon
1 teaspoon vanilla extract
4 slices of white bread (or brown bread or baguette, if you prefer)
50g butter
maple syrup, to serve

Beat the eggs, milk, sugar, cinnamon and vanilla together in a shallow bowl. Dunk the bread in it until well coated on both sides, but don't let it get too sloppy. Melt half the butter in a large frying pan, add the bread and fry gently on both sides until golden. Serve immediately, topped with the remaining butter and drizzled with maple syrup.

BACON

Now I know they say that bacon is bacon, but it was only when I arrived in England that I discovered the different cuts available here, and to my amazement the most common cut on the shelf was back bacon. Where I come from, and especially in my old neighbourhood, that would have been called ham and anything that meaty would have been served for dinner. If you are going to have a 'real' American breakfast, you need to use streaky bacon.

Place the bacon under a hot grill and grill – or broil, as we say back home – on both sides until slightly crisp. You will need at least 2 rashers per person. If you don't have a grill, then fry the bacon gently in a frying pan. You don't need to add any extra oil if you use streaky bacon, but if it's back bacon a little dab will do it. Use the fat for cooking other breakfast goodies, such as hash browns, eggs, grits, apples, and more.

FRIED HAM

If it comes from a pig, we'll eat it, and ham has always been a firm favourite. After cooking a large ham on the bone, you can simply cut off a few slices for frying. This is great for breakfast, lunch or dinner.

FOR 3–4

2 tablespoons vegetable oil
1 onion, thinly sliced
6 thick slices of good country ham, 8–10cm wide
salt and pepper

Heat the oil in a large frying pan, add the onion and fry over a medium heat for 3–4 minutes, until soft and lightly coloured. Add the ham, nestling it in between the onions, and season with salt and pepper. Fry for 3–5 minutes, until the ham begins to crisp up at the edges.

FRIED APPLES

Fried apples go well with a full country breakfast. They also make a tasty addition to any pork dish at dinnertime.

FOR 4–6

50g butter
5 cooking apples, cored and cut into eighths
   (I tend to leave the skin on, as it adds some
   texture, but you can peel them if you prefer)
100g soft brown sugar, or a touch more to taste
a little ground cinnamon
2–3 bacon rashers, cooked and chopped, or a
   handful of chopped ham (optional)

Heat the butter in a large frying pan, add the apples and fry gently, adding the sugar and cinnamon as soon as they begin to soften. The apples are ready when they are brown and soft – about 8–10 minutes should do it but be careful not to overcook them. Stir in the bacon or ham, if using, and serve.

HASH BROWNS

The good thing about hash browns is that almost everyone, young or old, will love them. The beauty of this recipe is that you can use leftover boiled potatoes, if you have any. Hash browns are great at lunch or dinnertime, but for me the best time is when you open your eyes in the morning to the smell of good old-fashioned 'home fries', as they are also called.

FOR 4–6

6 medium-sized potatoes, peeled and diced
4 tablespoons oil or fat for frying (bacon or sausage
   fat is best)
1 large onion, diced
1 tablespoon Momma's Cajun Seasoning (page 50)
salt and pepper

Put the potatoes in a large pan of water, season with a good pinch of salt, then bring to the boil and simmer until they are soft but not falling apart. Drain well and set aside. Now get a large frying pan and place it on the stove over a medium heat. Add the oil or fat. You can use vegetable oil but normally I would have already fried some bacon or sausages so I would use the same pan; it adds to the flavour. Then add the boiled potatoes, onion, Cajun seasoning and some salt and pepper. Stir all the ingredients together and fry for 8–10 minutes over a fairly high heat. It's nice when they get a bit of a crust, so don't rush them; let them do their thing and cook. Using a wooden spoon, gently turn the potatoes so that they are all coated with the seasoning and are crisp.

POTATO PANCAKES

I can remember waking in the morning to the smell of bacon and eggs and the sizzling sound of potato pancakes frying. There's no secret to this dish, it's just a good way to use up leftovers. It's similar to the British bubble and squeak, but without the cabbage.

leftover potatoes
a little finely chopped onion
bacon fat
salt and pepper

Just take any leftover potatoes and mash them with a fork, then add the onion and season with salt and pepper. Shape them into patties. Heat some bacon fat in a frying pan and fry the pancakes until they have a nice crust on both sides. Serve for breakfast, lunch or dinner.

COUNTRY OMELETTE

I've always found omelettes quite boring – unless, that is, they are packed with meat, vegetables and cheese, making them into a meal. My country omelette is just that – a fantastic meal on a plate, which can be served at any time of day or night.

FOR 2 (OR 1 VERY HUNGRY PERSON)

vegetable oil for frying
2 bacon rashers, chopped
50g chorizo sausage, chopped
2 tablespoons diced mixed red, green and yellow
    peppers
2 tablespoons diced onion
2 tablespoons chopped mushrooms
3 eggs
100ml milk
a pinch of Momma's Cajun Seasoning (page 50)
75g cheese, grated (Cheddar, blue, Swiss or
    American – you decide)
salt and pepper

Pour enough oil into a frying pan or omelette pan to coat the base, then place it over a medium heat. Add the bacon, chorizo, peppers, onion and mushrooms and fry until the bacon is done and the vegetables are tender. Whisk the eggs, milk, Cajun seasoning and some salt and pepper together. Pour them over the fried mixture and stir lightly to combine. Cook over a medium heat until set underneath, then sprinkle the cheese on top and gently fork it into the mixture. Place under a hot grill for 1 minute, or cover until the top sets, then turn the omelette on to a plate and serve.

CHEESE OMELETTE

Cook as above, but leave out all the meat and increase the quantity of cheese to 100–120g, depending on its strength.

CORNED BEEF HASH WITH POACHED EGGS AND SALSA

Now that you've made Hash Browns (page 24), you are ready to turn those potatoes into another delicious meal, corned beef hash. It's a real tasty dish done the back-home way.

FOR 2-4

4 medium-sized potatoes, peeled and diced
50ml vegetable oil
1 onion, diced
1 teaspoon finely chopped garlic
6 slices of corned beef (or a 340g can of corned beef)
8–10 cherry tomatoes
1 teaspoon vinegar
4–8 eggs (2 per person)
salt and pepper
Tomato Salsa (page 48), to serve
Cornbread, to serve (page 42)

Put the potatoes in a large pan of water, season with a good pinch of salt, then bring to the boil and simmer until they are soft but not falling apart. Drain well.

Heat the oil in a large frying pan, add the onion and garlic and fry gently until softened. Add the potatoes and some salt and pepper, stir well and fry for 8–10 minutes over a fairly high heat. Don't rush them – they need to get a bit of a crust. Crumble the corned beef over the potatoes, fold together and cook for 3–5 minutes. Add the cherry tomatoes and place under a hot grill for about 1 minute, to get a crust on the potatoes and to roast the tomatoes.

Meanwhile, bring a small pan of water to the boil and add the vinegar. Gently crack the eggs and drop them into the water (it's easier if you cook just 2 at a time). They will sink to the bottom but if you spoon the water over them this will help them keep their shape. They should be ready in about 2 minutes, so be careful not to overcook them. Remove from the pan and place in the centre of the hash. Top with Tomato Salsa – or ketchup. Serve with the hot buttered Cornbread.

TROPICAL FRUIT SMOOTHIE

This makes a wholesome treat for kids, a perfect non-alcoholic cocktail, or a refreshing drink for a hot summer's day. If you can't find all the fruits fresh, then use frozen fruit straight from the freezer, or even canned fruit.

FOR 8–10

1 mango, peeled, stoned and roughly chopped
$\frac{1}{2}$ small melon, peeled, seeded and roughly
   chopped
1 small punnet of blueberries
1 small pineapple, peeled and roughly chopped
   (or 1 small can of pineapple, drained)
100ml coconut milk
1 small papaya, peeled and roughly chopped
   (optional)
1 guava, peeled and roughly chopped (optional)
pulp and seeds of 4 passionfruit
1 banana, peeled and sliced
5 tablespoons Greek-style yoghurt
1 tablespoon honey
500ml cranberry juice
1 tray of ice cubes (for a juice-like cocktail) or 500ml
   vanilla ice cream (for a thick smoothie)

Whiz all the ingredients except the ice or ice cream in a blender for about a minute until smooth – do this in 2 or 3 batches, according to the size of your blender, then mix them together in a jug. Add the ice or ice cream to the final batch to make a brilliant smooth, icy drink.

SALADS
AND FIXIN'S

AVOCADO, TOMATO AND PEAR SALAD

COUSIN GORDON'S

SWEET POTATO SALAD

POTATO SALAD

DEVILLED EGGS

COLESLAW

RED CABBAGE SALAD

CORN SALAD WITH BLACK-EYED PEAS

FESTIVE APPLE SALAD

SWEET POTATO CRISPS

CORNBREAD

CORNBREAD STUFFING

HUSH PUPPIES

PICKLED CUCUMBERS

PINEAPPLE SALSA

GUACAMOLE

AMERICAN BLUE CHEESE DRESSING

TOMATO SALSA

CRANBERRY SAUCE WITH A HINT OF ORANGE

MOMMA'S CAJUN SEASONING

MOMMA'S CAJUN JERK SEASONING

AVOCADO, TOMATO AND PEAR SALAD

The first time I made this simple, tasty salad,
I acquired all the ingredients at a market, where
they were going cheap. They came to £3 in total
and I made enough salad to feed 50 people!
Here the quantities have been reduced to serve 4.

FOR 4

2 ripe avocados, peeled, stoned and diced
4 large, ripe pears, cored and diced
4 large tomatoes, cut into eighths
juice of 1 lemon
$\frac{1}{2}$ teaspoon sea salt
$\frac{1}{4}$ teaspoon cracked black pepper
4 tablespoons olive oil
a few iceberg or Little Gem lettuce leaves

Put the avocados, pears and tomatoes into a bowl
and pour over the lemon juice. Gently mix in the salt,
cracked black pepper and olive oil, then leave to
stand for about 15 minutes, until the flavours have
developed. Serve in the lettuce leaves.

COUSIN GORDON'S SWEET POTATO SALAD

When I first came to the UK in the late 1970s, I had to search high and low for sweet potatoes. They were available only in ethnic markets, among the African and West Indian foods. To my horror, I discovered that they weren't the same as the ones back home. Most of them had white, dry, stringy flesh rather than the moist, orange kind I was used to. I had to scratch the skin to make sure they were the variety I wanted. Well, thank God, things have changed now and you can find what I call the Southern American variety in almost every supermarket. The British have finally embraced one of my favourite vegetables and I can't wait to show you how to prepare them. When Gordon Ramsay visited my restaurant, even he got into the true soul spirit and showed me yet another way to serve the glorious sweet potato. I call it my Cousin Gordon's Sweet Potato Salad.

If you don't have any soured cream for the dressing, you can make your own, it's real easy. Get a pot of crème fraîche or double cream, squeeze in the juice of a lemon, add some salt and stir well.

FOR 4–6

4 orange-fleshed sweet potatoes, peeled and cut into slices 1cm thick
50ml olive or vegetable oil
1 tablespoon Momma's Cajun Seasoning (page 50)

For the soured cream dressing
250ml soured cream
50ml lemon juice
50g spring onions, sliced
$1/2$ teaspoon coarse sea salt
50g fresh coriander, finely chopped

Place the sweet potatoes in a pan of cold water, bring to the boil and simmer until tender. Be careful not to overcook them; the point of a knife should pass through them easily but they shouldn't be mushy. Remove from the pan with a slotted spoon. To make the dressing, simply put all the ingredients into a small bowl and gently stir together.

Pour the olive or vegetable oil into a hot frying pan and add the Cajun seasoning. When it has begun to cook gently, add the sweet potatoes and cook over a moderate heat until browned on both sides, being careful not to char the spices. Remove from the pan, arrange on a plate and top with the dressing.

WHEN GORDON RAMSAY VISITED MY RESTAURANT, EVEN HE GOT INTO THE TRUE SOUL SPIRIT AND SHOWED ME YET ANOTHER WAY TO SERVE THE GLORIOUS SWEET POTATO.

POTATO SALAD

There are a thousand and one different ways to make potato salad. Every country seems to have its own version. America has several, but in my neighbourhood we all tended to stick to the basic soul food recipe. This means adding a bit of sweetness, and in the UK I do this using a good-quality bought cucumber relish.

FOR 8

1.5kg waxy or new potatoes
100g celery, diced
100g onions, diced
100g mixed peppers, diced
240g mayonnaise
3 tablespoons mild American mustard
100g sweet cucumber relish
2 eggs, hard-boiled and chopped (optional)
paprika for sprinkling
salt and pepper

Don't ask me why, but somehow to get the best potato salad you need to boil the potatoes whole in their skins. When they are tender, drain well and leave until cool enough to handle. Peel them and dice into a large bowl (of course, if you are in a hurry you can peel and dice them before boiling). Add the celery, onions, peppers and some salt and pepper, then stir in the mayonnaise, mustard and cucumber relish. The jury is still out on whether boiled eggs should be included in a potato salad. I like them but I know a lot of people feel you don't need them, since there is always a devilled egg (below) next to it on the plate anyway. If you do decide to include the eggs, simply add them with the mayo. Sprinkle the salad with paprika and serve.

DEVILLED EGGS

Typically served on the side with potato salad (above) and coleslaw (opposite), these are also a great snack on their own.

FOR 12

6 eggs
2 tablespoons mayonnaise
1 teaspoon mild American mustard
1 teaspoon sweet cucumber relish
paprika for sprinkling
salt and pepper

Carefully add the eggs to a large pan of simmering water and cook for 10 minutes. Drain and run cold water over them to stop them discolouring. Peel the eggs and slice them lengthways in half. Scoop out the yolks and place in a bowl with the mayonnaise, mustard, sweet cucumber relish and some salt and pepper. Mix to a smooth paste, then use to fill the halved egg whites. Sprinkle with paprika.

COLESLAW

This is the way coleslaw is always prepared in my family. We like to add raisins and a touch of sugar.

FOR 6-8

1 small, firm white cabbage, cored and finely sliced
$1/2$ small red cabbage, finely sliced
1 onion, finely sliced
4 carrots, grated
100g raisins (optional)
250g mayonnaise
a dash of white vinegar
1 tablespoon caster sugar
salt and pepper

Put the white and red cabbage, onion, carrots and raisins, if using, in a bowl. Add the mayonnaise, vinegar, sugar and some salt and pepper and mix well. Leave to stand for about an hour, until all the flavours have fused.

VEGAN COLESLAW

Follow the recipe above but replace the mayonnaise with 4 tablespoons of lemon juice and 175ml olive oil.

RED CABBAGE SALAD

I first tasted this salad in a small taverna in Greece. It was prepared by an elderly woman who reminded me of my grandmother and her style of cooking.

FOR 4-6

1 red cabbage, cored and finely sliced
1 red onion, finely sliced
juice of 2 lemons
150ml extra virgin olive oil
salt and pepper

Combine all the ingredients in a bowl. Leave for at least 4 hours before serving.

CORN SALAD WITH BLACK-EYED PEAS

You can't get more soul than black-eyed peas. Combining them with sweetcorn turns them into a wonderful side salad.

FOR 4–6

2 x 325g cans of sweetcorn, drained
225g cooked black-eyed peas (canned ones are fine)
125g celery, finely diced
125g onions, finely diced
125g mixed peppers, finely diced
125g carrots, finely diced
50ml lemon juice
125ml olive oil
$\frac{1}{2}$ teaspoon salt
a pinch of cracked black pepper

Combine all the ingredients and leave for about an hour for the flavours to mingle. Turn the salad over from time to time to coat the vegetables fully.

FESTIVE APPLE SALAD

I have always loved salad. Yes, I know, I say that about most food, but a good salad can really make me sing. I love experimenting with different types of fruits, seeds and vegetables to come up with delicious healthy options. This recipe is a variation on the classic Waldorf salad. I've added a few extras to make it the perfect holiday salad.

FOR 4–6

2 Granny Smith apples, cored and diced
2 red dessert apples, cored and diced
1 tablespoon lemon juice
250g celery, diced
100g raisins
100g seedless white and red grapes, halved
2 satsumas, peeled and divided into segments
1 teaspoon white sugar
125g mayonnaise
1 teaspoon Momma's Cajun Seasoning (page 50)
2 Little Gem lettuces
100g walnuts or pecans, chopped

Place the diced apples in a large bowl and sprinkle with the lemon juice. Add the celery, raisins, grapes, satsumas, sugar and mayonnaise and toss together, making sure all the fruit is coated in the mayonnaise. Stir in the Cajun seasoning.

For a large, family-size salad, separate the lettuce leaves and arrange them around the edge of a large platter. Spoon the fruit mixture into the centre of the platter and sprinkle the nuts on top. Alternatively, for individual portions, place the lettuce leaves on small plates and put a heaped tablespoon of the fruit mixture into each one, then sprinkle with the nuts.

I HAVE ALWAYS LOVED SALAD.
YES, I KNOW, I SAY THAT ABOUT MOST
FOOD, BUT A GOOD SALAD CAN REALLY
MAKE ME SING.

SWEET POTATO CRISPS

These make a lovely snack served with Soured Cream Dressing (page 34). They are also wonderful as a topping for soups.

2 medium-sized sweet potatoes (1 orange-fleshed and 1 white-fleshed)
vegetable oil for deep-frying
salt or Momma's Cajun Seasoning (page 50) – for savoury crisps
2 tablespoons caster sugar mixed with 1 tablespoon ground cinnamon – for sweet crisps

With a potato peeler, thinly peel the sweet potatoes and then peel the flesh into thin strips. Save the peelings, as these can also be deep-fried. Place in a bowl of ice-cold water and leave for about an hour. Pour off the water and pat the sweet potatoes dry on kitchen paper. Try to remove as much of the water as possible; if you drop dripping-wet sweet potatoes into hot oil, the oil will start to pop all over the place and you may burn yourself.

Pour some vegetable oil into a deep-fat fryer or a deep saucepan and heat to about 190°C. Fry the sweet potatoes in small batches, along with the peelings, until golden brown – this should take a matter of seconds. Carefully lift them out of the hot oil with a slotted spoon and place on kitchen paper to drain. Then sprinkle with salt, Cajun seasoning, or sugar mixed with cinnamon. The crisps can be stored in an airtight container for up to 2 days.

CORNBREAD

This is the first type of bread that comes to mind when planning a soul food menu. It dates back to the Native American Indians, who used ground corn for cooking before the European explorers arrived. Cornbread was popular during the American Civil War because it was very cheap and could be made in various different forms – baked into high-rise, light, fluffy loaves or muffins, or quickly fried into patties such as Hush Puppies (page 44). Any leftover cornbread can be frozen to use in stuffings (opposite) or Meatloaf (page 74), or deep-fried as croûtons.

FOR 6-8

225g butter
225g plain flour, sifted
225g medium yellow cornmeal
1 tablespoon baking powder
1 teaspoon salt
125g caster sugar (optional, but better if you add it; cornbread should be a little sweet)
2 large eggs
475ml milk (preferably full-fat, but semi-skimmed is also good)

Set the oven to 180°C/Gas Mark 4. Put the butter in a 23cm round or square baking tin (or a 12-cup muffin tin) and place in the hot oven to melt, being careful not to let it burn. Remove once melted.

Combine all the dry ingredients in a bowl and make a well in the centre. Add the eggs, milk and melted butter and stir well with a wooden spoon, working fast so that the butter doesn't harden. Pour the mixture into the warm baking tin, place in the oven and bake for 35–40 minutes, until risen and golden brown. Serve immediately – with butter and jam, if you have a sweet tooth. It's also good with a fried breakfast, or with meat or fish, or on its own.

THIS IS THE FIRST TYPE OF BREAD THAT COMES TO MIND WHEN PLANNING A SOUL FOOD MENU.

CORNBREAD STUFFING

Back home, depending on where you come from, stuffing is sometimes known as dressing, but whatever you call it, it conjures up fond memories of family gatherings at Thanksgiving and Christmas and what goes inside your big bird. My mother used a simple mixture of stale bread, a bit of veg and butter to stuff our holiday bird. Nowadays stuffings have taken on a whole new vibe. No longer is it just a bird thing. Stuffings for fish, meats, and vegetables are common, and sometimes stuffings are even baked separately, outside the bird, to keep vegetarians happy.

Seafood, meat, fruit, nuts and vegetables can all be used in a variety of stuffings. If you are making a traditional bread stuffing, make sure the bread is stale. This is easy to do: just leave a few slices of bread out overnight and crumble them, or put cubed bread in a very low oven for about 15 minutes.

This recipe combines stale bread and cornbread. Whenever I bake cornbread, I always put at least 6 pieces aside for freezing (they keep well in the freezer). When I need them, I defrost them and warm them through for immediate eating, or leave them out in the open air to go stale for my stuffing.

FOR 6–8

150g butter
1 onion, diced
1 green pepper, finely diced
1 red pepper, finely diced
4 celery stalks, finely diced
1 garlic clove, finely chopped
2 teaspoons Momma's Cajun Seasoning (page 50)
$\frac{1}{2}$ teaspoon salt
$\frac{1}{4}$ teaspoon ground black pepper
1 tablespoon dried sage
25g fresh coriander (stems and leaves), chopped
4 slices of stale white or brown bread
6 pieces of stale Cornbread (opposite), each 7–8cm square
250–300ml chicken or vegetable stock
100g cranberries (optional)
50g walnuts (optional)

Melt the butter in a large frying pan over a medium heat, then add all the diced vegetables, plus the garlic, Cajun seasoning, salt, pepper and herbs. Stir well and cook until the onion is translucent. Crumble the stale bread and cornbread into the mixture and combine well. Add the stock a little at a time, until the mixture is moist and holds together. Stop adding the stock before it gets too wet – it should be firm enough for you to mould with your hands. You can stir in the cranberries and nuts at this stage, if using. The mixture is now ready for stuffing into birds, fish or vegetables, or you can place it in a buttered ovenproof dish and bake in an oven preheated to 180°C/Gas Mark 4 for about 20 minutes. Be careful not to let it dry out.

HUSH PUPPIES

After making cornbread, you can mix any remaining batter with leftover vegetables from the main meal to create little fritters, known as hush puppies. Traditionally, these were fried on top of the stove, using the leftover fat in the pan. There are plenty of stories about the origins of the name. Many believe it comes from the Deep South, where cooks would shout, 'Hush, puppies' as they threw scraps out into the back yard to keep the dogs from barking at the smells coming from the kitchen.

MAKES 15–20

$1/4$ quantity of Cornbread batter (page 42), kept back
　　from baking
1 small onion, chopped
$1/2$ each red, green, and yellow pepper, finely
　　chopped
$1/2$ teaspoon dried chilli flakes
a touch of crushed garlic
4 tablespoons drained canned sweetcorn
1 teaspoon Momma's Cajun Seasoning (page 50)
$1/2$ teaspoon salt
$1/4$ teaspoon black pepper
300ml vegetable oil

Mix the batter with all the remaining ingredients except the oil. Heat the oil in a large, deep pan, then drop dessertspoonfuls of the batter into it, taking care not to overcrowd the pan. Fry gently, turning twice, until the fritters have risen up and browned. The smell should fill your home with goodness. Serve with Fried Catfish Goujons (page 54).

COOKS WOULD SHOUT, 'HUSH, PUPPIES' AS THEY THREW SCRAPS OUT INTO THE BACK YARD TO KEEP THE DOGS FROM BARKING AT THE SMELLS COMING FROM THE KITCHEN.

PICKLED CUCUMBERS

I don't know about you but I find cucumber a very boring vegetable. Most people just slice them into a salad. Of course, you can also jazz them up by pickling them. We have eaten sweetened pickled cucumbers at family gatherings for years. They are very quick to make, and so delicious that it takes the boring out of cucumbers.

FOR 4–6

2 cucumbers, peeled and thinly sliced
1 onion, thinly sliced
100g caster sugar
125ml cider vinegar

Put the sliced cucumbers and onion in a bowl, sprinkle the sugar over them and pour over the vinegar. Toss together until well coated, then leave to marinate for at least 1 hour – the longer the better. The cucumbers will begin to release their juices. Serve with Potato Salad (page 36) or as a side salad to any main course.

PINEAPPLE SALSA

Every time we turn around these days, we're given a new sauce to try. There are countless salsas on the market now. Well, I'm no different, I have come up with a very simple 5-minute salsa using pineapple and chilli as a base. It has a fresh, cooling flavour and tastes great piled on top of Fried Catfish Goujons (page 54) or served with meaty fish such as salmon or red snapper.

250g fresh pineapple, cut into chunks (or 1 can of pineapple chunks, drained)
a pinch of dried chilli flakes
2 tablespoons finely chopped fresh coriander
a pinch of salt
a squeeze of lemon juice

Put all the ingredients in a bowl. Mix with a hand blender until the salsa is quite smooth but still has some texture; don't over blend it.

GUACAMOLE

Believe it or not, I'd never eaten an avocado until I went to live in Mexico in 1971. They grew on the trees over there like apples do back home. At first I couldn't understand the fascination with them, and it took a while before I would even try them. Now I eat avocados whenever I can get my hands on them, and use them to make soups, sauces and salads. My favourite way of eating avocados is as a guacamole dip to serve with tortilla chips or fajitas (page 84).

FOR 4-6

2 ripe avocados
1 small onion, finely diced
1 garlic clove, finely chopped
1 small tomato, diced
$1/2$ teaspoon Momma's Cajun Seasoning (page 50)
$1/2$ teaspoon dried chilli flakes
juice of 1 lime or $1/2$ lemon
salt and pepper

Peel the avocados and remove the stones. Using a fork, mash the avocado flesh in a bowl. Mix in the onion, garlic and tomato, then add the seasoning, chilli flakes and lime or lemon juice. Serve chilled.

AMERICAN BLUE CHEESE DRESSING

I tend to use an English blue cheese or Roquefort for this dressing. Whatever you choose, it must be strong flavoured, with a crumbly texture. Serve with Hot Buffalo Chicken Wings (page 90), or use as a dressing for your favourite salad.

FOR 4-6

1 garlic clove, peeled
$1/2$ teaspoon sea salt
1 tablespoon lemon juice
1 teaspoon balsamic vinegar
2 tablespoons olive oil
150ml soured cream

2 tablespoons mayonnaise
40g blue cheese, crumbled
$1/2$ teaspoon Momma's Cajun Seasoning (page 50)
$1/4$ teaspoon black pepper

Crush the garlic clove to a paste with the salt, then mix with the lemon juice, vinegar and oil. Stir in the soured cream and mayonnaise. When it is all blended together, add the crumbled blue cheese, Cajun seasoning and black pepper. Cover and chill overnight.

TOMATO SALSA

When I was 16, I spent a year living in Mexico as an international exchange student. I became fascinated by the different ways of making tomato salsas, both raw and cooked. This is one of my favourite cooked versions.

FOR 8–10

1 red, 1 green and 1 yellow pepper, roughly chopped
2 large onions, roughly chopped
1–2 fresh red chillies, roughly chopped
1 garlic clove, peeled
100ml olive oil
1kg tomatoes or 2 x 400g cans of whole plum
   tomatoes, drained
1 tablespoon salt
1 teaspoon ground cumin
1 teaspoon cumin seeds
a handful of fresh coriander, chopped
juice of 1 lemon and 1 lime, plus a little of the grated
   zest

Place the peppers, onions, chillies and garlic in a large baking tin, pour the olive oil over them and place on the top shelf of an oven preheated to 220°C/Gas Mark 7. Roast for 20–30 minutes, until the vegetables are beginning to blacken.

Meanwhile, dip some kitchen paper in olive oil and use to wipe the base of a heavy-bottomed frying pan so it is lightly coated. Place the pan over a high heat and, when it is hot, put the whole tomatoes in their skins (or the drained plum tomatoes) in it. They will begin to sizzle, pop and darken. Cook for at least 5 minutes, until they are almost black underneath but still red and juicy inside. Turn them over with a wooden spoon and keep cooking until they are blackened all over. Peel off the skin if using fresh tomatoes. Add the tomatoes to the tin of roasted vegetables, sprinkle over the salt and cumin and roast for 15–20 minutes in the middle of the oven.

Remove from the oven and transfer to a bowl, making sure you scrape the baking tin well. So that you don't lose any of the goodness and flavour, add a little water to the tin and stir well to loosen the bits that have stuck to the base, then add this to the vegetables. Leave to cool, then stir in the fresh coriander and the lemon and lime juice and zest. Use a hand blender to chop everything roughly and blend it together. You can add more chilli at this stage if you prefer it hotter. Serve the salsa over nachos, with fajitas (page 84), or as an accompaniment. It will keep in the fridge for up to a week.

CRANBERRY SAUCE WITH A HINT OF ORANGE

For me, it's not holiday season without cranberry sauce to go with the turkey. I always used to buy mine readymade until my Aunt Carolyn showed me how quick and easy it is to make at home.

FOR 4-6

275g cranberries
100g granulated sugar
120ml water
25g butter
grated zest of 2 oranges

Put the cranberries, sugar and water in a pan and bring to the boil. Simmer for 10–15 minutes, until the cranberries pop open, then stir in the butter and orange zest. Leave to cool, then chill overnight. Serve with turkey or other meats.

MOMMA'S CAJUN SEASONING

Most of my recipes call for Cajun seasoning and although you can buy it, homemade is always best. That way you can experiment each time until you get the blend and the degree of heat to your personal taste. A Cajun seasoning mix is basically salt with a variety of spices. Use it as you would salt, being careful not to add too much salt to dishes that contain Cajun seasoning. Heat weakens spice flavours, so avoid displaying the seasoning on a shelf near the cooker.

You can order my Cajun Seasoning online at www.soulinabowl.com.

10g ground cayenne pepper or chilli powder
10g ground black pepper
10g ground garlic powder
10g ground coriander
10g ground cumin
7g dried chilli flakes
7g white sugar
60g dried onion flakes
25g dried mixed herbs
7g grated nutmeg
50g salt

Put the ground spices and all the other ingredients except the salt into a food processor or spice grinder and blend to a fine consistency. Be careful not to breathe it in, as it will get you sneezing. Mix the blended seasoning with the salt and store in a jar. It should keep for at least a month – or you can store it in the freezer if you want to keep it for longer.

MOST OF MY RECIPES CALL FOR CAJUN SEASONING AND ALTHOUGH YOU CAN BUY IT, HOMEMADE IS ALWAYS BEST.

MOMMA CHERRI'S CAJUN JERK SEASONING

Invented by the Arawak Indians, the original natives of Jamaica, jerk seasonings are traditionally found in the Caribbean Islands. There are many recipes for them, both wet and dried. The word jerk refers to a seasoning blend, a cooking method, and the meat that has been jerked. It is not part of my soul food past but, having lived in England for almost 30 years, I have absorbed many Caribbean influences on my cooking. Shopping in the open markets, I can't help but discover new and exotic foods.

When I first came to England I was part of a soul-pop band, Ray Shell and the Street Angels. We came from all over the world and, before a gig, we would all cook up some down-home foods. My good friend and singing companion, Andrea, came from Barbados, and her special contribution was her mother's version of a wet jerk seasoning for chicken or fish and fried saltfish cakes. She would select the finest ingredients and spend hours preparing them. I have never had the patience to sit and chop for hours, so I watched and learned, then came up with my own short cuts. I don't claim to know all the secrets of jerk seasoning but I believe my simple recipe does the trick.

1 bunch of spring onions, roughly chopped
1 bunch of flat-leaf parsley, roughly chopped
2 tablespoons roughly chopped fresh coriander
1 lime
1 red or yellow Scotch bonnet chilli, chopped
juice of $\frac{1}{2}$ lemon
about 2 tablespoons olive oil
a pinch each of sea salt and black pepper
1 teaspoon Momma's Cajun Seasoning (page 50)
a pinch of ground mixed spice
plenty of time and love for the mixing

Put the spring onions, parsley and coriander into a bowl. Using a sharp knife, peel the lime, cutting close to the flesh to remove all the white pith. Cut it in half and take out the pips. Add the lime halves to the bowl with half the chopped chilli. Depending on how hot you want it, you can discard the seeds from the chilli. Using a hand blender, mix together the ingredients in the bowl. Squeeze in the lemon juice, then slowly pour in the olive oil while still mixing so it all blends together nicely. Mix in the salt, pepper, Cajun seasoning and mixed spice. The mixture should be fairly smooth but not puréed. Taste it and add the other half of the chilli if you want it hotter. You can use the seasoning straight away but the flavour improves the longer it sits. I tend to leave it in the fridge to chill. You are now ready to use it to stuff or rub into your fish or chicken (pages 62 and 92), or as a spicy marinade seasoning for vegetables and salads.

FISH

FRIED CATFISH GOUJONS
CAJUN-STYLE
CATFISH GUMBO
MOMMA'S SPICY FISHCAKES
FISH JAMBALAYA

FRIED JERK RED SNAPPER
BLACKENED CAJUN FISH
(OR CHICKEN) FILLETS
CRAB CAKES
GARLIC AND CHILLI
TOMATO KING PRAWNS
DRUNKEN PRAWNS

FRIED CATFISH GOUJONS

Fried catfish has always been a traditional soul food item but it is fairly new to the UK. The meaty, white-fleshed fish has a delicate but distinctive flavour. When it is prepared as goujons – tender, sweet pieces of fish fillet coated in cornmeal – children seem to prefer it to processed fish fingers, and why not?

You might have to search for catfish but when you do find it you'll be very happy. A good fishmonger should be able to get hold of it for you. Alternatively some Oriental shops sell frozen catfish fillets, often under the name pangasius. If you can't find any catfish then cod or haddock make a good alternative.

FOR 2-4

75g cornmeal
35g plain flour
a pinch each of salt and pepper
a pinch of Momma's Cajun Seasoning (page 50)
4 fresh or frozen catfish fillets, skinned, then either
   left whole or cut into strips for goujons
about 100ml vegetable oil
Pineapple Salsa (page 46), to serve

Combine all the dry ingredients in a bowl. Wash the fish and then coat it in the dried mixture. Pour the oil into a large frying pan and place it over a moderate heat. Put the fish in the pan skin-side down – i.e. the side that would have had the skin on it, not the rounded side. Cook over a moderate heat for 1$\frac{1}{2}$–2$\frac{1}{2}$ minutes per side for goujons, 3–5 minutes for whole fillets. Serve with Pineapple Salsa together with Hush Puppies (page 44), Hoppin' John (page 103), Coleslaw (page 37) and greens.

MY MOTHER DOESN'T LIKE FISH, AND AS A RESULT WE NEVER ATE IT AT HOME.

Instead we had to go to our Aunt Delia and Uncle Albert's house down the street. Uncle Albert and other menfolk would take my brothers, and occasionally the girls, fishing or crabbing in Delaware at weekends and on their return we'd have a big fry-up.

IF IT WAS SUMMER, WE WERE IN LUCK, BECAUSE WE'D BE DOWN SOUTH AT MY GRANDPARENTS' HOUSE AND MY GRANDDADDY LOVED FISH. I'VE KNOWN HIM EAT IT FOR BREAKFAST, LUNCH AND DINNER.

It's funny because I love catfish now, can't get enough of it, but growing up I wouldn't go near it. They are such ugly fish, with whiskers. I remember being chased around the yard once by one of the older boys flinging a big, ugly, slimy, scary catfish at me!

CAJUN-STYLE CATFISH GUMBO

Once you discover the beauty of catfish, you will soon begin to use it in a whole variety of dishes. Adding it to a gumbo, as stews are often referred to in the South, turns it into a one-pot meal – or you can serve it as a fish soup to start a meal. If you can't find catfish, you could substitute a nice, meaty piece of cod or haddock.

FOR 6

120g butter
100g plain flour
1 onion, finely chopped
2 celery stalks, finely chopped
1 red and 1 green pepper, diced
2 garlic cloves, crushed
400g can of chopped tomatoes
$1/_2$ teaspoon salt
$1/_4$ teaspoon crushed black pepper
$1/_4$ teaspoon dried chilli flakes
1 teaspoon Momma's Cajun Seasoning (page 50)
475ml water (or vegetable stock)
400g can of sweetcorn, drained
100g mushrooms, sliced
500g fresh (or frozen) okra, trimmed and sliced
    lengthways in half
4 fresh or frozen catfish fillets, skinned

Melt the butter in a deep frying pan, stir in the flour and cook over a low heat for a minute or two to make a smooth roux. Add the onion, celery, diced peppers and garlic and cook over a low heat for 4–5 minutes, until soft and tender. Stir in the tomatoes, salt, pepper, chilli flakes, Cajun seasoning and water, then cover and simmer for 15 minutes. Add the sweetcorn, mushrooms and okra and continue to cook for 15 minutes, Lay the fish fillets on top of the vegetables and simmer for 5 minutes, until the fish is done. Break the fish up into chunks and stir to combine it with the other ingredients, trying not to mash it up too much. Serve with plain rice.

MOMMA'S SPICY FISHCAKES

Fishcakes are quick and easy to make and a great way to use up leftovers. If you have leftover cooked potatoes and fish you can mix them with the seasonings below and hey presto!, spicy fishcakes in a jiffy.

MAKES ABOUT 20

4 medium potatoes (about 750g), peeled and cut
    into chunks
300g fresh or frozen catfish fillets, skinned, or some
    nice meaty fillets of cod or haddock
1 onion, finely chopped
a handful of fresh coriander, finely chopped
1 teaspoon Momma's Cajun Seasoning (page 50)
$\frac{1}{2}$ teaspoon dried chilli flakes, or 1 fresh chilli, finely
    chopped
2 tablespoons mild American mustard
1 teaspoon salt
$\frac{1}{2}$ teaspoon freshly ground black pepper
vegetable oil for frying

For coating
100g cornmeal
50g plain flour
salt and pepper

Cook the potatoes in boiling salted water until tender, then remove from the pan with a slotted spoon and place in a bowl, reserving the cooking water. Mash them thoroughly.

Cut the catfish fillets into smaller pieces. Put them in the hot potato-cooking water, cover the pan and leave for about 3 minutes; the fish should poach in the heat of the water. If it needs a little more cooking, simply return the pan to the heat and bring back to a simmer, then remove and leave uncovered for another 3 minutes. Don't overcook the fish or it will begin to toughen. Drain off the water (you can freeze this in an ice-cube tray, if you like, and use, a cube at a time, to add fishy flavour to other dishes). Leave the fish until cool enough to handle, then add it to the mashed potatoes with the onion, coriander, Cajun seasoning, chilli, mustard and salt and pepper. Gently stir together. Mix the cornmeal and flour together on a shallow plate and season with salt and pepper. With floured hands, shape the fish mixture into medium-sized patties and gently coat them in the cornmeal mixture. Place on a floured plate and put them into the fridge to chill for at least 1 hour – the longer the better. This helps the fishcakes hold together during cooking.

Pour enough oil into a large frying pan to coat the base and place it over a medium heat. When the oil is hot, add the fishcakes, in batches if necessary, and fry gently for about 1–2 minutes on each side, until they form a golden-brown crust. Serve with sweet chilli sauce and together with Cajun Potato Wedges (page 128) and Hush Puppies (page 44).

FISH JAMBALAYA

This is very similar to the meat version on page 76 but uses a wonderful assortment of fish. My favourites are cod, smoked haddock, catfish, snapper, salmon and king prawns. You can, of course, use whatever fish you prefer. All the fillets should be cut into nice large pieces – about 6 chunks each.

FOR 6–8

about 200g smoked haddock fillet
about 200g cod fillet
about 200g catfish fillet
juice of 1 lemon
3 tablespoons Momma's Cajun Seasoning (page 50)
3 tablespoons vegetable or olive oil
2 onions, 1 roughly chopped, 1 thinly sliced
1 red, 1 green and 1 yellow pepper, half of each diced and the other half cut into strips
1 teaspoon crushed garlic
1 tablespoon ground cumin
1 teaspoon cumin seeds (optional, but it adds a nice touch if you have them)
1 teaspoon salt
$1/2$ teaspoon ground black pepper
1 chilli, preferably Scotch bonnet, seeded and finely chopped, or left whole
400g easy-cook American-style rice
1 teaspoon turmeric
450g mixed vegetables, e.g. 1 carrot, diced, 1 courgette, diced, a handful of peas, a handful of green beans and a few broccoli and cauliflower florets (or you could use a small bag of frozen mixed vegetables)
1.2 litres water or fish stock
1 teaspoon gumbo filé (if you have it)
500g peeled raw king prawns or crayfish
a handful of mushrooms, sliced

Skin the fish fillets and cut them into large dice. Sprinkle the lemon juice and 1 tablespoon of the Cajun seasoning over them and set aside to marinate while you cook the jambalaya.

Place a large saucepan over a medium heat and add 1 tablespoon of the oil, followed by the chopped onion, diced peppers and crushed garlic. Stir in 1 tablespoon of the remaining Cajun seasoning and half the cumin, plus the salt and pepper. Cover and cook over a low heat for about 5 minutes, until the onion and peppers have softened. The spices will begin to give off their fragrance and coat the pan, which will enhance the dish. I call this seasoning the pot. Now stir in half the marinated fish, plus the chopped fresh chilli. Remember that Scotch bonnet chillies are very hot; if you have any cuts they will burn you. If you are worried about the heat level, a useful tip is to leave the chilli whole and add it to the dish with the water or stock, removing it after 10 minutes. Its unique flavour will be released but the heat will be kept to a minimum.

Add the rice and stir well, then add the turmeric and the remaining Cajun seasoning and cumin. Stir everything together until the rice is fully coated, then add the mixed vegetables and the water or fish stock. Bring to a simmer and add the gumbo filé, if using. Simmer, uncovered, over a low heat for 20 minutes. When the rice has swollen and is almost cooked, add the prawns or crayfish and simmer for a further 5–10 minutes, until the shellfish are cooked. Adjust the seasoning according to taste – you might want to add a touch more chilli.

Now for the final ingredient, the stir-fried fish. Heat the remaining 2 tablespoons of oil in a large frying pan, add the remaining marinated fish and stir-fry for 5 minutes. Add the sliced onion, peppers and mushrooms and stir-fry for 2 minutes, until the fish is cooked through and the vegetables are tender. Place on top of the jambalaya and serve immediately.

IT'S SO FUNNY BECAUSE WHEN WE WERE YOUNGER MY BABY BROTHER CURT ONLY ATE PEANUT BUTTER AND JELLY SANDWICHES AND COLD BREAKFAST CEREAL.

Seriously, that's all he ever ate. My mother was at her wit's end, trying to make sure he didn't melt away.

SOMEHOW, HE MANAGED TO SURVIVE ON JUST THAT, UNTIL HE DISCOVERED THAT HE LOVED THE ONE THING MY MOTHER HATED AND NEVER HAD IN THE HOUSE... FISH.

Who would have thought that Curt would take such a huge culinary jump in taste? He's no longer a baby and his love of seafood continues to amaze me. The Pan-Fried Jerk Red Snapper on page 62 is one of his favourites.

PAN-FRIED JERK RED SNAPPER

Fish is always a number one option for my baby brother, Curt, and he is keen to try out all sorts. He loves whiting, sardines and catfish, and although he doesn't lean towards spicy food, he can't get enough of my stuffed Jerk Red Snapper. This recipe is a great summer dish as it is nice served hot or cold and can be altered to accommodate almost any type of fish, just as long as it is meaty enough to be sliced and stuffed. This is great when served alongside Hoppin' Johns (page 103), Fried Plantain (page 127) and Sweet Potato Salad (page 34).

FOR 2–4

1 tablespoon Momma Cherri's Cajun Jerk Seasoning
   (page 51) for each fillet
2–4 red snapper fillets, 2–3cm thick

For the stuffing
2 teaspoons Momma Cherri's Cajun Jerk Seasoning
   for each fillet

For the cornmeal coating
75g cornmeal
35g plain flour
a pinch each of salt and pepper
a pinch of Momma's Cajun Seasoning (page 50)

about 100ml vegetable oil

Rub the Cajun jerk seasoning into the fish fillets. Make an incision in each fillet and stuff about 2 teaspoons of jerk seasoning into it.

Combine all the ingredients for the seasoned cornmeal coating in a bowl. Take each fillet and coat it in the dried mixture. Pour enough oil into a large frying pan to cover the base and place it over a moderate heat. If you prefer, you can omit the coating and simply cook the fish on a griddle pan for 3–5 minutes on each side, depending on the thickness. If you are cooking a lot of fish, it's easier to roast the whole lot in a hot oven for 8–10 minutes.

BLACKENED CAJUN FISH (OR CHICKEN) FILLETS

Blackening does not mean burning your food. It is a way of seasoning it. If you rub some Cajun or dried jerk seasoning over fish or meat, then quickly fry it in melted butter over as high a heat as you can manage, it will sear the spices and create a crust, producing the blackened effect. Don't worry if you can't get the crust to form at first; it takes a little practice. If your meat or fish is more than 2.5cm thick, you will need to finish it off in the oven to ensure it is cooked through properly.

Any firm-fleshed fish will work, as long as it is at least 1.2cm thick. Try red snapper, salmon, tuna, shark, etc. Remember that the frying pan will become very hot, so take care, and use protective gloves. The melted butter could flame up, so never leave the pan unattended. Cook no more than two pieces of fish or meat at a time and season immediately before placing them in the pan. If cooking more than one batch of fish or meat, wipe the pan clean with paper towels after each one so that the seasoning doesn't build up and give the food a burnt rather than a blackened effect; there is a difference!

FOR 2

3 tablespoons butter
2 x 200g fish fillets (or 2 chicken breast fillets)
2 tablespoons Momma's Cajun Seasoning (page 50)

Melt the butter in a frying pan over a medium heat and add the fish or chicken, turning to coat it in the butter on both sides. Now take the fillets out of the pan and quickly coat them in the Cajun seasoning. Return them to the pan and turn up the heat. If you are using fish, cook for 3–4 minutes on each side, depending on thickness. If you are using chicken, cook for 3–4 minutes on each side and then finish it off in an oven preheated to 180°C/Gas Mark 4 for 8–10 minutes. You can add more butter if necessary.

CRAB CAKES

In the summer months my brother, Craig, and I were the privileged ones because, as the two oldest children, we were allowed to go crabbing in Delaware or Maryland with our neighbours. We used to have so much fun. We had to leave in the early hours of the morning, while it was still dark, so that we could arrive at daybreak when the waters were calm. We would lower our lines into the water and sit on the dock of the bay, eating saltine crackers and sandwiches and waiting for a bite on our lines. When a crab was caught, that's when the fun began because, to tell the truth, we both loved going but deep down inside we were afraid of the crabs. Part of our job was to place them in a large bucket, and make sure they didn't escape. As a result, we were often nipped by their claws. Although I didn't like them, I would take pride in chasing my brother around with a live crab trying to nip him. Those were the good old days, when children knew how to entertain themselves.

FOR 4

500g fresh crabmeat
1 onion, finely chopped
1 egg
1 teaspoon Momma's Cajun Seasoning (page 50)
1 teaspoon Worcestershire sauce
1 teaspoon mild American mustard
2 teaspoons chopped parsley
$1/2$ teaspoon salt
$1/4$ teaspoon ground black pepper
1 teaspoon lemon juice
100g fresh breadcrumbs or 100g Cornbread (page 42), crumbled
vegetable oil for shallow-frying

Put all the ingredients except the vegetable oil in a large bowl and combine well. If the mixture is too dry, add a touch of milk, just so it is moist enough to form into patties. Gently shape into about 12 patties, about 7.5cm across, and place on a tray lined with greaseproof paper. Place in the fridge and chill for at least an hour. This will help the crab cakes hold their shape.

When you are ready to cook them, place a large frying pan on the heat and add enough oil to cover the base. When the oil is hot, add the crab cakes and cook for 3–4 minutes on each side, until browned. Serve with rice, potatoes or salad.

I WOULD TAKE PRIDE IN CHASING MY BROTHER AROUND WITH A LIVE CRAB TRYING TO NIP HIM. THOSE WERE THE GOOD OLD DAYS, WHEN CHILDREN KNEW HOW TO ENTERTAIN THEMSELVES.

GARLIC AND CHILLI TOMATO KING PRAWNS

I love prawns, whether peeled or in their shells, grilled, baked, fried, any way they come. Serve this lively dish as a starter, or as a main course with rice, noodles or salad.

FOR 4–6

1kg king prawns, peeled and de-veined
1 head of garlic, peeled and roughly chopped
1 teaspoon Momma's Cajun Seasoning (page 50)
4 tablespoons olive oil
1 onion, diced
1 tablespoon dried chilli flakes
2 tomatoes, diced
juice of 1 lemon

Place the peeled prawns in a bowl with the garlic, Cajun seasoning and 1 tablespoon of the olive oil and mix well. Leave to marinate for at least an hour.

Heat the remaining olive oil in a large frying pan and add the onion and chilli flakes. When the onion begins to cook, add the prawns and garlic and quickly stir together. Cook for about 2 minutes, until the prawns start to go pink, then add the chopped tomatoes and squeeze the lemon juice over. Cook for another minute, remove from the heat and serve immediately.

DRUNKEN PRAWNS

This dish can be found in the Deep South and on several Caribbean islands. I usually serve it in the restaurant on special occasions. Many recipes use beer but I prefer to use a nice dark rum. I figure if you're gonna get those prawns 'drunk', then do it with rum!

Needless to say, this is not one of my family recipes. My mum turns her nose up at the very idea of it. She doesn't drink, and shies away from anything on a menu containing alcohol, but that's her and not me. Bring it on, I say!

FOR 4-6

1kg medium to large prawns, peeled and de-veined
100ml dark rum
150ml pineapple juice
2 teaspoons finely chopped garlic
1 tablespoon chilli sauce or Tabasco sauce
100g fresh coriander, chopped
1 teaspoon Momma's Cajun Seasoning (page 50)
1 tablespoon soft dark brown sugar

This is one of the easiest dishes to make. Simply place all the ingredients except the sugar in a bowl and leave to marinate for at least an hour. Then pour the lot into a shallow frying pan and gently bring to the boil. Cook for just a few minutes, until the prawns are firm and pink, then remove them from the pan and set aside. Add the brown sugar to the juices and simmer until the mixture has reduced and thickened. Add another splash of rum and return the prawns to the pan, tossing them in the drunken juices. Serve them on their own or over a bed of rice.

MANY RECIPES USE BEER BUT I PREFER TO USE A NICE DARK RUM. I FIGURE IF YOU'RE GONNA GET THOSE PRAWNS 'DRUNK', THEN DO IT WITH RUM!

MEAT

PHILLY CHEESE STEAK

POOR MAN'S PIE

MEATBALLS

HOMEMADE BURGERS

MOMMA'S MEATLOAF

MOMMA'S MEAT

JAMBALAYA

SOUTHERN-FRIED PORK CHOPS

SMOTHERED PORK CHOPS

WITH ONIONS AND APPLES

PIG'S TROTTERS
CHITTERLINGS
SOUTHERN-STYLE CHICKEN
AND CHORIZO FAJITAS
REV. DAISY'S
SOUTHERN-FRIED CHICKEN
HOT BUFFALO
CHICKEN WINGS
GRILLED OR BAKED JERK CHICKEN
BARBECUE CHICKEN
BROTHER BRIAN'S BBQ RIBS
ROAST TURKEY

PHILLY CHEESE STEAK

I was born and bred just outside Philadelphia and if you came from that neck of the woods you grew up eating Philly cheese steaks. They are sold on most street corners. When you find a good one, you tell all your friends where you got it and you will be prepared to travel miles for that return visit.

Cheese steaks were invented in the 1930s at Pat's Steaks in South Philadelphia, hence the name, Philly. I never leave home – that is, Philly – without having had a good cheese steak. It should have American cheese, Provolone or Cheez Whiz (a yellow processed cheese squeezed from a bottle) on it. I have discovered that if you top it with grated mild English Cheddar you won't be far off the mark. It can be served plain or with fried onions, sweet and hot chillies and salad.

FOR 2 (OR 1 VERY HUNGRY PERSON)

275g steak, sliced into strips (as thinly as possible, so the steak cooks quickly and remains tender)
a 30cm piece of soft baguette, or two 15cm hotdog rolls
100–150g mild Cheddar cheese, grated
salt and pepper

Optional additions
1 small onion, thinly sliced
1 small green pepper, thinly sliced
a handful of mushrooms, thinly sliced

Place the steak in a hot frying pan and sauté quickly until done to your liking. Season to taste with salt and pepper. If you want to serve it with onion, pepper and mushrooms, then either fry them separately in a little oil or fry them with the meat – in which case you won't need any oil. If you fry them separately, place them on top of the meat in the roll before the cheese goes on.

Briefly warm the bread, place the cooked steak in it and top with the cheese. Place under a grill to melt the cheese (or you can stir the cheese into the steak at the end of cooking before placing it in the roll). From start to finish, it should take no more than 10 minutes.

I WAS BORN AND BRED JUST OUTSIDE PHILADELPHIA AND IF YOU CAME FROM THAT NECK OF THE WOODS YOU GREW UP EATING PHILLY CHEESE STEAKS.

POOR MAN'S PIE

I invented this dish as a hearty winter filler for the restaurant. It is loosely based on shepherd's pie, with a Southern twist. I usually make it on a Monday, when I have leftover mashed potatoes. When I was a child, my mother used to do a similar dish with a cobbler topping. I've changed the recipe by topping it with cornbread.

FOR 6–8

4 medium-sized potatoes, peeled and chopped (or 450g leftover mash)
50g butter
120–150ml milk
500g minced beef
1 onion, diced
1 garlic clove, finely chopped
1 green and 1 red pepper, diced
1 teaspoon salt
$1/2$ teaspoon pepper
1 teaspoon Momma's Cajun Seasoning (page 50)
4 chorizo sausages, sliced or diced
1 teaspoon dried chilli flakes (optional)
2 tablespoons plain flour
200g can of sweetcorn, drained
1 sweet potato, peeled and cut into 1cm dice
$1/2$ quantity of Cornbread batter (page 42)

Cook the potatoes in boiling salted water until tender, then drain well, reserving the cooking water. Mash with the butter and enough milk to give a smooth texture, then season to taste and set aside.

Now move on to the meat. Place the mince in a large frying pan over a medium heat to brown it off. I tend not to add any oil to the pan, as the beef will release its own fat. Once the meat has browned, add the onion, garlic and peppers, then stir in the salt, pepper and Cajun seasoning and cook for 10 minutes. Stir in the chorizo, and the chilli flakes if you want an added kick, and give it a good stir. Once the meat is cooked, pour off any excess fat, leaving just a little in the pan. Make a well in the centre of the mixture and stir the flour into the remaining fat to make a simple roux. Now gradually stir in 500ml of the potato water. I like to discard the top part of the water, leaving just the bottom half, which contains a lot of the potato starch and helps to thicken the gravy. Stir in the sweetcorn and sweet potato and cook over a low heat for 10 minutes, until the potato is tender.

Transfer the mixture to an ovenproof dish and top with the mashed potatoes, then spread the cornbread mixture over the potatoes. Place the dish in an oven preheated to 180°C/Gas Mark 4 and bake for 30–40 minutes, until the cornbread has risen and cooked through; the topping is ready when a knife inserted in the centre comes out dry and clean.

MEATBALLS

Meatballs are quick and easy to make and are a great way of introducing children to cooking, since you can let them help shape the mixture. Serve with potatoes and other vegetables, or in a hotdog or burger bun as a lunchtime snack.

FOR 6-8

1 onion, peeled
1 green pepper
1 mild chilli
800g minced beef
50g fresh coriander (leaves and stalks), chopped
2 tablespoons Momma's Cajun Seasoning (page 50)
1 teaspoon salt
$^1/_2$ teaspoon black pepper
1 tablespoon Worcestershire sauce
1 egg

Barbecue Sauce (page 96), gravy or tomato sauce, to serve

Cut the onion, green pepper and chilli into chunks, put them in a bowl and blend them together with a hand blender (if you don't have a hand blender, just chop them finely). Add the mince, coriander, seasonings, Worcestershire sauce and egg and mix well with your hands. Shape the mixture into balls, slightly smaller than a golf ball. Place on a baking tray and bake in an oven preheated to 180°C/Gas Mark 4 for 20 minutes. Serve with Barbecue Sauce, tomato sauce or gravy, plus potatoes and vegetables.

HOMEMADE BURGERS

I don't like to add a lot of extras to my burgers. I believe it's what you put on top that makes a good burger, not all the extras in the meat. These are meaty burgers, which will rival those from any of the high-street outlets. Try these and the kids will want to stay at home for their weekend treat.

MAKES 8

1kg minced beef
1 teaspoon salt
$^1/_2$ teaspoon black pepper
2 tablespoons Momma Cajun Seasoning (page 50)
1 tablespoon Worcestershire sauce

To serve
sliced onions, peppers and tomatoes
lettuce leaves
pickles
slices of cheese

Put all the ingredients for the burgers in a bowl and mix with your hands. Shape into 8 patties and then cook on a hot griddle pan for 2–3 minutes on each side. Unlike steak, I believe burgers should be thoroughly cooked. Top each burger with onions, peppers, tomatoes, lettuce, pickles and cheese. Serve with Cajun Potato Wedges (page 128) or in a bun.

MOMMA'S MEATLOAF

The popular saying is 'as American as apple pie' but it might just as well be meatloaf, especially in soul food. It's one of those dishes that embodies the soul of our nation: good, honest, home-cooked food, made with love and care. There are many variations on meatloaf, some including lots of chunky vegetables and some without. I like to include the vegetables but I chop them up in a food processor first, or use a hand blender to reduce them to a fine pulp. This way it saves the kids from moaning that they don't want any, or sitting there picking them out. I remember my daughter sitting for hours at the table, taking her meals apart and discarding any visible vegetables.

A hand blender is a useful kitchen tool and not at all expensive. It may not be the Rolls-Royce of equipment, but believe me, it does the job.

FOR 6-8

900g minced beef
2 onions, peeled
2 garlic cloves, peeled
1 green pepper
1 red pepper
1 celery stalk
6 pieces of stale Cornbread (page 42), or 4 slices of stale white bread
3 eggs
2 tablespoons Worcestershire sauce
2 tablespoons American mustard
1 teaspoon salt
$1/2$ teaspoon black pepper
1 tablespoon Momma's Cajun Seasoning (page 50)
1 teaspoon dried chilli flakes (optional)
3 tablespoons chopped coriander
2 teaspoons dried mixed herbs
12 streaky bacon rashers

Place the minced beef in a large bowl and set aside. If you don't have a hand blender or food processor, you will need to chop all the vegetables finely by hand, but the easiest way to make a good meatloaf is to chop them into rough chunks, then put them in a bowl and blend them together with a hand blender. Crumble in the cornbread or bread and add the eggs, Worcestershire sauce, mustard, salt, pepper, Cajun seasoning, chilli flakes, if using, coriander and mixed herbs. The mix should be quite sloppy and wet. Make sure your hands are clean, because I believe the best way to make meatloaf is to get your hands into the mix. Pour the chopped vegetable and bread mixture into the mince and combine well. Once the mixture is completely blended, shape it into 6 oval meat loaves, about the size of a balled-up fist. Wrap each one in streaky bacon by crisscrossing 2 rashers over it, then place on a baking tray. Alternatively, you can line two 900g loaf tins with the bacon rashers, then press the meatloaf mixture into them. Place in an oven preheated to 180°C/Gas Mark 4 and bake for 40 minutes for the small loaves or 1 hour for the larger ones. Serve with mashed potatoes and green beans.

IT'S ONE OF THOSE DISHES THAT EMBODIES THE SOUL OF OUR NATION: GOOD, HONEST, HOME-COOKED FOOD, MADE WITH LOVE AND CARE.

MOMMA'S MEAT JAMBALAYA

This has become, as they say, my signature dish. Jambalaya is a rice dish that was first served in New Orleans. You can find similar dishes all over the world. Believe it or not, I never made or even ate jambalaya until I decided to open my restaurant in Brighton. Then I did a lot of research into different ways of preparing it and came up with my own European soul version. I have also developed fish and vegetarian jambalayas (pages 60 and 105). The beauty of this easy dish is that you can substitute or add whatever you like. It's a great way to use up what's in your kitchen.

A true jambalaya contains gumbo filé, a greenish powder that comes from the sassafras tree, which is native to America. It is not readily available in the UK but if you are travelling to the southern states of America you will find it there. I often have problems myself finding it up north in America. There are some online suppliers that can deliver straight to your door, not least my own site, www.soulinabowl.com. Do order some, as you need only a small amount in this dish, and you will then have plenty left over to add to gumbos and soups.

FOR 6–8

4 chicken breasts (I prefer them skinned but you could leave the skin on, if you like)
juice of 1 lemon
3 tablespoons Momma's Cajun Seasoning (page 50)
3 tablespoons vegetable or olive oil
2 onions, 1 roughly chopped, 1 thinly sliced
1 red, 1 green and 1 yellow pepper, half of each diced and the other half cut into strips
1 teaspoon crushed garlic
1 tablespoon ground cumin
1 teaspoon cumin seeds (optional, but it adds a nice touch if you have them)
1 teaspoon salt
$1/2$ teaspoon ground black pepper
4 chorizo sausages, skinned and sliced
1 chilli, preferably Scotch bonnet, seeded and finely chopped, or left whole
400g easy-cook American-style rice
1 teaspoon turmeric
450g mixed vegetables, e. g. 1 carrot, diced, 1 courgette, diced, a handful of peas, a handful of green beans and a few broccoli and cauliflower florets (or you could use a small bag of frozen mixed vegetables)
1 litre water or chicken stock
1 teaspoon gumbo filé (if you have it)
500g peeled raw king prawns or crayfish
a handful of mushrooms, sliced

(continued on page 78)

THIS HAS BECOME, AS THEY SAY, MY SIGNATURE DISH.

(continued from page 76)

First of all, you need to prepare the chicken. If you look at other recipes for jambalaya, you will notice that the raw chicken is usually added at the beginning and cooked with the rice. I find the chicken tends to stew if you do this, and the texture isn't as juicy as it should be. So I marinate it, then stir-fry it separately and add it at the end. So, cut the chicken breasts into thin strips. Sprinkle over the lemon juice, then 1 tablespoon of the Cajun seasoning, and set aside to marinate while you cook the jambalaya.

Place a large saucepan over a medium heat and add 1 tablespoon of the oil, followed by the chopped onion, diced peppers and crushed garlic. Stir in 1 tablespoon of the remaining Cajun seasoning and half the cumin, plus the salt and pepper, then add the chorizo. Cook for about 5 minutes, until the onion and peppers have softened and the chorizo begins to release some of its juices. The spices will give off their fragrance and coat the pan, which will enhance the dish. I call this seasoning the pot.

Now stir in the chopped fresh chilli. Remember that Scotch bonnet chillies are very hot; if you have any cuts they will burn you. If you are worried about the heat level, a useful tip is to leave the chilli whole and add it to the dish with the water or stock, removing it after 10 minutes. Its unique flavour will be released but the heat will be kept to a minimum.

Add the rice and stir well, then add the turmeric and the remaining Cajun seasoning and cumin. Stir everything together until the rice is fully coated, then add the mixed vegetables and the water or chicken stock. Bring to a simmer and add the gumbo filé, if using. Simmer, uncovered, over a low heat for 20 minutes. When the rice has swollen and is almost cooked, add the prawns or crayfish and simmer for a further 8–10 minutes, until the shellfish are cooked. Adjust the seasoning according to taste – you might want to add a touch more chilli.

Now for the final ingredient, the stir-fried chicken. Heat the remaining 2 tablespoons of oil in a large frying pan, add the chicken and stir-fry for 2 minutes. Add the sliced onion, peppers and mushrooms and stir-fry for 3 minutes more, until the chicken is cooked through and the vegetables are tender. Place on top of the jambalaya and serve immediately.

BELIEVE IT OR NOT, I NEVER MADE OR EVEN ATE JAMBALAYA UNTIL I DECIDED TO OPEN MY RESTAURANT IN BRIGHTON. THEN I DID A LOT OF RESEARCH INTO DIFFERENT WAYS OF PREPARING IT AND CAME UP WITH MY OWN EUROPEAN SOUL VERSION.

SOUTHERN-FRIED PORK CHOPS

We have a long tradition of eating nearly every part of the pig, dating back to the time when slaves were given pork off-cuts to cook with. For me, the tastiest meat comes from a pig. I love to pick up one of these pork chops in my hands and chew away until I have devoured every last bit of succulent meat. It's one of those dishes where you will see nothing left on the plate but the bones!

FOR 4

60g plain flour
30g cornmeal (fine or coarse)
2 tablespoons Momma's Cajun Seasoning (page 50)
4 pork chops (bone-in are best, but loin chops are good too)
150ml vegetable oil
1 onion, thinly sliced
1 green pepper, thinly sliced
200ml water

Put the flour, cornmeal and 1 tablespoon of Cajun seasoning into a large plastic bag or on a large plate, and shake/mix together. Rinse the pork chops and season both sides with the remaining tablespoon of Cajun seasoning. Coat them in the flour mixture, making sure they are evenly covered.

Heat the oil in a large frying pan, add the chops and fry over a medium heat for 5–8 minutes, depending on thickness. Turn the chops over, spread the sliced onion and green pepper on top and cover the pan. When the chops are browned underneath, remove the lid and pour off the excess oil. Turn the chops over again, while stirring the onion and pepper, and add 1 tablespoon of the flour mixture. Mix in the flour, then slowly stir in the water. Continue to cook for 2 minutes. The chops should have a nice coating, with a gravy-like onion and pepper mixture to go on top. Add a little more water, if necessary. Serve with mashed potatoes.

SMOTHERED PORK CHOPS WITH ONIONS AND APPLES

This recipe was inspired by my grandmother. On a busy day she would simply throw everything into a pot and stick it in the oven to slow roast. I have added mushrooms because I think they go well with pork and apples.

FOR 4–6

2 tablespoons vegetable oil
4–6 pork loin chops (not too thin), weighing about 900g in total
2 onions, sliced
1 green pepper, sliced
250g mushrooms, sliced
1 teaspoon soy sauce
1 teaspoon Momma's Cajun Seasoning (page 50)
4 large cooking apples, cored and quartered
2 tablespoons soft brown sugar
salt and pepper

Heat the vegetable oil in a large frying pan, add the pork chops and brown on both sides. Transfer to a large baking tray and sprinkle with salt and pepper.

Add the onions, pepper, mushrooms and soy sauce to the pan and sauté for 1 minute. Add 2 tablespoons of water, let it bubble, then spread the mixture over the pork chops. Sprinkle the Cajun seasoning on top. Cover with a lid or foil and place in an oven preheated to 180°C/Gas Mark 4. Bake for 20 minutes, then remove the lid or foil and top with the apples and brown sugar. Continue to cook for 20–30 minutes, until the apples are tender. Do not stir; the pork chops should be smothered in the vegetables and apples. Serve with mashed potatoes and green beans.

PIG'S TROTTERS

I grew up in a neighbourhood where the smell of pig's feet and chitterlings (opposite) cooking would draw a crowd. Pig's feet, or trotters as they are known here in Britain, can be found in most high-street butchers. If you don't see them, simply ask. Trust me, they'll be there, and you won't believe how cheap they are. I have had them prepared in many different ways but I always come back to this simple, down-home method of just boiling them in a pot.

FOR 3–4

6 pig's trotters
120ml vegetable oil
4 litres water
1 medium-sized ham hock (optional)
1 onion, peeled
1 red and 1 green pepper
1 chilli
1 head of garlic
3 celery stalks, with their leafy tops
4 bay leaves
2 tablespoons salt
1 teaspoon black peppercorns
1 teaspoon paprika
2 teaspoons Cajun seasoning
1 potato
chilli sauce and cider vinegar, to serve

If there are any hairs on the trotters, burn them off with a lighter or, even easier, over the flame of a gas cooker. Wash and scrub them until they are clean, making sure you clean well between the toes, because when they are cooked you will want to suck all the meat off – yes, even from the toes!

Heat the oil in a large pot, add the trotters and cook over a high heat until browned all over. Carefully pour off the hot oil, then add half the water. Bring to a rapid boil and continue to boil for at least 10 minutes, regularly skimming off the froth as it rises to the surface. Then add all the remaining ingredients, including the extra 2 litres of water. Keep the onion, peppers, chilli and garlic whole. Legend has it that if you cook a whole potato with trotters or chitterlings, they won't smell as much while simmering. Lower the heat, cover and simmer for at least $2\frac{1}{2}$ hours, until the meat begins to fall from the bones. I often add a ham hock to the pot. Although trotters are delicious, they don't tend to have a lot of meat on them, so the ham hock helps to bulk out the dish and gives everyone a little extra meat on their plate.

Serve the trotters topped with a chilli sauce of your choice (I like any American smooth red sauce), sprinkled with cider vinegar and accompanied by Potato Salad (page 36) and greens.

I GREW UP IN A NEIGHBOURHOOD WHERE THE SMELL OF PIG'S FEET AND CHITTERLINGS COOKING WOULD DRAW A CROWD.

CHITTERLINGS

Chitterlings are by far my favourite food in the world, but it's no good telling you that if you don't know what they are. Chitterlings are pig's intestines. Before you can even begin to cook them, you must make sure they are thoroughly cleaned. We all know what passes through the intestines, so if you are lucky enough (or unlucky enough) to get fresh ones you must go through the long process of cleaning them. Because chitterlings are such a popular dish in America, they can be found ready cleaned and frozen in most specialist supermarkets. Even so, you need to give them a final wash. I'm not even gonna pretend they smell good while they're cooking. They stink – let's face it, they once contained all the waste materials from the pig.

Cooking chitterlings is an art. Back home, some people are famous for knowing how to cook a mean batch. My cousin, Norma, prepared some of the best chitterlings in town. She cleaned them so well, we would all joke that she bleached them, and the smell while they were cooking was minimal. Chitterlings are usually cooked at holiday time or on special occasions. My mother always gets a big batch in when I return home to the States. You need to buy plenty, as they reduce greatly in size. After long, slow cooking, they should be eaten with plenty of hot sauce and vinegar.

FOR 6-8

5kg chitterlings (hopefully pre-washed and cleaned)
2 large onions, cut in half
1 head of garlic, cut in half
1 large potato, peeled but left whole
3 celery stalks, coarsely chopped
100g fresh sage
20g salt
50g black peppercorns
2 tablespoons dried chilli flakes
2 carrots, roughly chopped

Let's assume you have a batch of cleaned chitterlings. Cleaned or not, you should wash them again, so hold them under a running tap and pass the water through them, pulling and squeezing to remove all dirt and leftover muck. Then cut the chitterlings into 6cm strips and place in a large pot. Cover with water and bring to the boil. Simmer for at least 10 minutes, then drain well. Rinse the chitterlings and return them to the pot. Add all the vegetables and seasonings, plus enough water to cover. Cover with a lid and slowly bring to the boil. Simmer for $3^1/_2$–4 hours, until the chitterlings are tender. They will reduce in volume a lot. That's the main problem with them, you think you have a big pot full and when they are finished you end up with only about half of what you thought you had.

Once they are cooked, remove them from the water with a slotted spoon. Serve with hot sauce and vinegar, Potato Salad (page 36), Cornbread (page 42) and greens.

...BY FAR MY FAVOURITE FOOD IN THE WORLD...

SOUTHERN-STYLE CHICKEN AND CHORIZO FAJITAS

America is a melting pot when it comes to food, and Mexico has contributed some of the wonderful spices found in our dishes. Soul food in particular has been influenced by our Latin cousins, from Mexico, Central and South America and the surrounding Caribbean islands.

The chicken in these fajitas can be replaced by fish, prawns or vegetables – just make sure you spice them up.

FOR 4-6

juice of 1 lemon
4 chicken breasts, skinned and cut into thin strips
2 tablespoons Momma's Cajun Seasoning (page 50)
2 chorizo sausages, sliced
1 onion, finely sliced
1 green, 1 red and 1 yellow pepper, finely sliced
50g mushrooms, sliced
1 courgette, sliced
200g fresh or canned baby sweetcorn (optional)
3 tablespoons vegetable oil
1 teaspoon ground cumin
1 teaspoon dried chilli flakes (optional)
1 packet of soft flour tortillas
Tomato Salsa (page 48)
Guacamole (page 47)
soured cream

Sprinkle half the lemon juice over the chicken, then a tablespoon of the Cajun seasoning, mix and set aside. Toss the chorizo and vegetables with the remaining lemon juice and seasoning.

Place a large frying pan over a medium heat and add 2 tablespoons of the oil. When hot, add the sliced chicken, ground cumin and the chilli flakes, if using, and stir-fry for 3 minutes. Add the sliced chorizo and vegetables and continue to stir-fry for about 5 minutes, until the chicken is cooked through. You may need to do this in 2 batches; if so, keep the first batch warm in a moderate oven while you get on with the rest.

Warm the flour tortillas in the oven (or in the microwave for 10 seconds). Divide the chicken and chorizo mixture between the tortilla and top with Tomato Salsa, Guacamole and soured cream. Roll up and enjoy the flavours of Mexico, soul food style.

ONE OF MY EARLIEST MEMORIES IS OF SITTING ON MY DADDY'S LAP, SUCKING THE MARROW OUT OF A FRIED CHICKEN BONE.

By the time I was five my mother was a single parent and every summer, to give her a break, my brothers, sister and I were shipped off to the southern state of Virginia, where we stayed with my maternal grandparents, along with any cousins who had also made the trip. I use to love my stays in the country. We were all too young to understand about segregation, and we played happily without a care in the world. When we got older, new laws came into place and things changed considerably. We no longer had to ride at the back of buses or drink from separate fountains.

We were a close family and each summer we would hold large reunions, where all the women would set about cooking up a soulful storm.

MY GRANDMOTHER WAS KNOWN FOR FRYING UP SOME OF THE BEST CHICKEN IN THE WORLD.

Sunday was the day when you knew you would be well fed. I have early memories of waking to the smells of a busy kitchen, including the aroma of fried chicken. We spent most of the day in church, and because it was such a long day the women would all contribute to the after-service meal. Church was deep in the countryside, miles away, so there was no way we could go home and then come back. Once you arrived for Sunday school at 9am you were stuck there, sometimes until 6pm. Unfortunately, if you were under 16 that didn't guarantee you a full plate.

WE KIDS WOULD STAND TO THE SIDE, LICKING OUR LIPS IN EAGER ANTICIPATION OF A PIECE OF CHICKEN.

I used to get so annoyed when I saw half-eaten bits of chicken on the grown-ups' plates with nothing set aside for us. But my grandmother would always make sure we had a little something to chew on.

AFTER ALL, IF WE WERE EXPECTED TO ENDURE ANOTHER 2 HOURS OF CHURCH, WE NEEDED SOME FOOD TO STOP THE RUMBLE IN OUR BELLIES.

REV. DAISY'S SOUTHERN-FRIED CHICKEN

Fried chicken can be found on almost every soul food table. There is no mystery to its preparation or cooking at all. Because I was the oldest child and my mother always worked, I had to learn to cook from an early age. There were no cookbooks, I just stood and watched, and was often left to finish off a dish. Fried chicken was one of the first things I learned to cook. We never went to the commercial takeaway places. Why would we, when we knew there was always a skillet of fresh chicken frying at home?

FOR 4-6

10 chicken pieces (I prefer legs, thighs and wings, as
   they tend to be the juiciest)
1 teaspoon salt
1 lemon
2 tablespoons Momma's Cajun Seasoning (page 50)
1 teaspoon ground black pepper
1 teaspoon garlic powder
200g plain flour
500ml vegetable oil for frying
1 tablespoon butter

For the chicken gravy
3 tablespoons seasoned flour (from the bag you use
   to season the chicken pieces)
1 tablespoon light soy sauce or 1 teaspoon gravy
   granules (optional, but it does help)
1 litre water, chicken stock or vegetable stock
whisky, rum or tequila (optional)

Wash the chicken pieces and gently pat them dry. Sprinkle with the salt, then squeeze over the juice from the lemon and sprinkle with half the Cajun seasoning, black pepper and garlic powder. Leave to rest for at least 10 minutes. If you are planning a large meal, you can cover the chicken and leave to marinate overnight in the fridge.

When you are ready to cook, place the flour in a large plastic bag for shaking, or in a bowl, and mix in the remaining seasonings. Add the seasoned chicken pieces to the flour mixture and toss until fully coated. Heat the oil in a large, deep frying pan, preferably cast iron, and add the butter (I always include a touch of butter if my oil is fresh and it's the first time frying; it helps to brown the chicken and adds extra flavour). To test the temperature of the oil, drop a pinch of flour in it; if it begins to sizzle immediately, you can begin frying. Place the coated chicken pieces skin-side down in the pan and cook for 5–8 minutes over a medium heat, until golden brown. Turn the pieces, cover the pan and cook for 6–10 minutes, then uncover the pan and turn the chicken again. Continue to fry until the chicken is cooked right through to the bone; the juices should run clear if you insert a knife. Remove the chicken from the pan and drain on kitchen paper. Keep warm while you make the gravy.

Pour the oil from the pan into an empty tin or jar, leaving the meat drippings behind for the gravy. (Save the oil for the next time you fry chicken. I find a mixture of half pre-used oil and half fresh oil fries the best – this way you don't need to add the butter to the oil for flavour and colour.) Place the frying pan over a moderate heat and stir in the 3 tablespoons of seasoned flour. After about a minute, when it begins to brown, add the soy sauce or gravy granules, if using, followed by the water or stock (if you are boiling potatoes, their cooking water makes the best gravy). Bring to the boil, then reduce the heat and simmer until reduced to the consistency you like. To jazz up the gravy, you can add a little of your favourite alcoholic drink with the water or stock – I've tried whisky, rum and tequila.

Serve the fried chicken with the gravy. Mashed potatoes make the best accompaniment.

See opposite for a couple of Southern-fried variations.

SOUTHERN-FRIED JERK CHICKEN

Sprinkle the chicken pieces with salt and pepper, then use a small, sharp knife to make a 3cm-long cut in the fleshiest part of each one, creating a small pocket. Stuff each one with a teaspoon of Momma Cherri's Cajun Jerk Seasoning (page 51) – this creates a little surprise when you bite into the chicken. If you like it really hot, push a little seasoning under the skin too. Toss the chicken pieces in the mixture of flour, salt, pepper, Cajun seasoning and garlic powder used for Southern-Fried Chicken and cook as described opposite.

SOUTHERN-FRIED CHICKEN NUGGETS

Follow the recipe on the opposite page but substitute 2–3 skinned boned chicken breasts, cut into 5cm cubes. Cook as above for 6–10 minutes. I often make these nuggets for children, in which case I tend not to marinate the chicken, as it makes them too spicy.

HOT BUFFALO CHICKEN WINGS

Chicken wings used to be left on the bird, to be used in soups, gravy, stock or just thrown away. The story goes that a woman named Teressa Bellissimo, who ran a bar in Buffalo, New York, invented this recipe in 1964. Chicken wings became an overnight hit because of the fiery sauce, celery sticks and blue cheese dressing, but most of all because they no longer had to be thrown away. There are many recipes for the hot sauce but the one given below is the one used in my neighbourhood back home.

Some people believe that the wing tips should be removed and the wings cut at the joints in order for them to be called buffalo wings. Cutting them into smaller pieces makes them easier to eat and share.

FOR 4

10 chicken wings
2 tablespoons Momma's Cajun Seasoning (page 50)
200g plain flour
1 teaspoon salt
1 teaspoon black pepper
1 litre vegetable oil for deep-frying
3 celery stalks, cut into thin strips about 7.5cm long
250ml American Blue Cheese Dressing (page 47)

For the sauce
125g butter
a 57ml bottle of Crystal Hot sauce or Tabasco sauce
   (it's important to use an American-style smooth,
   hot sauce, not a Caribbean pepper sauce)

To make the sauce, slowly melt the butter in a pan and stir in the hot sauce. Gently cook the butter and hot sauce together for at least 10 minutes.

Cut the wings at their joints, sprinkle with a tablespoon of the Cajun seasoning and set aside for 10 minutes. Put the flour, salt, pepper and remaining Cajun seasoning in a large plastic bag and add the wings, shaking to coat them. Dust off any excess. Heat the oil to 180°C in a deep-fat fryer or a deep saucepan. Fry the chicken wings, a few at a time, for 5–10 minutes, until they are crisp and cooked through (the juices should run clear when a sharp knife is inserted). Remove and drain on kitchen paper. Place the wings in a dish and pour the hot sauce over them. Serve as a starter or snack, accompanied by the celery and the blue cheese dressing for dipping. The celery and dressing help soften the heat of the spicy sauce.

GRILLED OR BAKED JERK CHICKEN

Jerk chicken and jerk fish have slowly but surely made their way on to my menu. I have taken my recipe for jerk seasoning back home to America and served it to my mother: she won't touch the fish but loves the chicken!

As I've already mentioned, jerk seasoning is not traditionally associated with American soul food. I've spent so much time in England and have enjoyed and absorbed so many traditional Caribbean recipes, that, inevitably, these flavours and methods have been adopted into my own recipes.

Don't be put off by the inclusion of chilli peppers and spice in the marinade, they add a lot of flavour to the dish and not necessarily heat. Give it a try, but remember to take it easy at first, begin with a little seasoning and increase as your taste buds take to the overall warmness of the dish.

FOR 6–8

½ quantity of Momma Cherri's Cajun Jerk Seasoning (page 51)
6–10 chicken pieces or 20 chicken wings

Rub the jerk seasoning into the chicken pieces and leave to marinate in the fridge for at least 1 hour, preferably overnight.

Place the chicken skin-side down on a hot ridged griddle pan and cook over a fairly high heat for 8–10 minutes. Turn the pieces over and reduce the heat to medium. Cover with a lid or foil and cook for another 10 minutes. Uncover and turn again, then continue to cook until the juices run clear when you insert a skewer. Alternatively, if you want to bake the chicken, seal it first by placing it on the hot griddle for about 2 minutes per side, then transfer it to an oven preheated to 180°C/Gas Mark 4 and cook for 15–20 minutes.

I HAVE TAKEN MY RECIPE FOR JERK SEASONING BACK HOME TO AMERICA AND SERVED IT TO MY MOTHER: SHE WON'T TOUCH THE FISH BUT LOVES THE CHICKEN!

If you prepare a large quantity of Barbecue Sauce (page 96), you can make a variety of meat and vegetable dishes. In Caribbean cooking you find a lot of curried dishes but us American soul folks tend to lean towards the barbecue.

THERE IS A LONG TRADITION OF SMOKED AND BARBECUED MEATS ON OUR TABLES.

Perhaps this dates from the time when much of our cooking was done outside on open fires and in smokehouses. From an early age, I remember the menfolk taking over the grills and barbecue pits.

AT FAMILY REUNIONS AND PICNICS, WHILE THE WOMEN WERE BUSY INSIDE FRYING CHICKEN AND BAKING CAKES AND PIES, THE MEN WOULD GRAB A COLD DRINK, PUT ON AN APRON AND MAKE THEIR WAY TO THEIR DOMAIN – THE OUTSIDE BARBECUE PIT. HERE'S WHERE THE RIBS, CHICKEN, PORK, FISH AND EVEN SOME VEGETABLES WOULD EITHER GET BURNT TO A CRISP OR GRILLED TO PERFECTION.

I would recommend that you buy a cast-iron ridged griddle pan, as it will add to the overall flavour of any dish. Even if I am cooking outside on a barbecue grill, I tend to begin all my meats indoors. You have to be careful when barbecuing that everything is cooked through to the bone. Many a barbecue has been spoilt by underdone meat and it's just not worth ruining your day – and everybody else's, if they get sick from eating raw meat. Starting the cooking indoors might seem like cheating but it will save you time in the end and it also means you can relax and enjoy yourself in the knowledge that everything has been properly cooked.

BARBECUE CHICKEN

There are so many ways to prepare chicken. Southern-fried (page 88) is my favourite but barbecue chicken comes a very close second. You can find a variety of dried barbecue seasonings to add to the mix. You might also want to add a little curry powder. Remember, with soul food it's about experimenting with what you already have in your cupboard. There's no right or wrong way, simply your way.

FOR 4

1 teaspoon salt
$1/2$ teaspoon black pepper
1 chicken, cut into eighths, or 8 pre-cut chicken
   pieces
2 tablespoons soft brown sugar
4 tablespoons white vinegar or cider vinegar
1 tablespoon Momma's Cajun Seasoning (page 50)
juice and grated zest of 2 oranges
1 tablespoon dried barbecue seasoning or $1/2$
   tablespoon smoked paprika (optional)
Barbecue Sauce (page 96)

Rub the salt and pepper into the chicken pieces, followed by the brown sugar, vinegar, Cajun seasoning, orange juice and zest, and barbecue seasoning or paprika, if using. Cover the chicken and leave to marinate for at least 1 hour, or overnight in the fridge.

Place a ridged griddle pan on the stove and turn the heat up to maximum. Once the pan is red hot, take the chicken pieces out of the marinade and shake off any excess liquid. Place them skin-side down on the griddle and cook for about 3 minutes, until scored underneath. Be careful because there will be a lot of smoke and the meat will begin to sizzle. Turn the chicken over and cover with a large lid or a piece of foil (this will help give it a smoky flavour). Reduce the heat and cook for 5 minutes, until sealed underneath. You now have two options: you can transfer the chicken to a roasting tin and cook it in an oven preheated to 190°C/Gas Mark 5 for 10–15 minutes, then take it outside to your barbecue grill and finish off by brushing with the barbecue sauce and grilling for 5–10 minutes. This is merely to combine the flavours of the sauce with the meat – the chicken will have already cooked in the oven. Of course, if you're competent on an outside grill you can cook the chicken on it from raw but do make sure it's cooked right through. I prefer to pre-cook my meat for peace of mind. Alternatively you can spread the barbecue sauce over the chicken after its 10–15 minutes in the oven and return it to the oven for 5–10 minutes, until the sauce has browned and is beginning to bubble. Either way, your meat should be tender and juicy, with a wonderful barbecue flavour.

VARIATIONS

You can now go on to prepare many other ingredients in the same fashion: pork chops, turkey portions and even fish fillets or whole fish.

In 2001, when my husband, Phil, and I decided to open Momma Cherri's in Brighton, we interviewed only one chef and that was Brian Moyo. We hit it off on so many levels that we knew immediately we would be able to have a great working relationship.

TOGETHER WE DEVELOPED AND ENHANCED SOME OF THE OLDEST AND SIMPLEST DISHES – DISHES WE BOTH USED TO EAT GROWING UP.

I was amazed at how much we had in common. Brian's childhood was spent in Africa, with parents from Zambia and Zimbabwe, while I grew up in the States. Like mine, his grandmother was the strong figurehead of a large, close family. I feel I have been truly blessed because I grew up in a loving, supportive family. It saddens me when I hear of families who don't get together and support each other. We did this regularly through our family reunions, holidays, and any other excuse we could use to meet up.

FROM THE START, I KNEW THAT BRIAN COULD COOK. OVER THE YEARS HE GREW INTO THE HEAD CHEF I ALWAYS HOPED I WOULD HAVE.

For five years, Brian gave his all, but in 2006 he decided to step down as head chef. He generously passed on his knowledge of soul food to the new chef, Tristan Dooley. He worked with Tristan to help him understand and develop the soul food concept. He leaves us to return to his love of art – those hands that so lovingly mixed meatloaf and breaded chicken for all those years will now be busy creating in a new way. He might be gone, but his recipe for BBQ Ribs (page 96) lives on at the restaurant.

BROTHER BRIAN'S BBQ RIBS

Brian may be gone from the restaurant's kitchen but his legendary recipe for BBQ ribs, which have been known to have grown men licking their fingers in public, stays with us. They are so moist, with meat that just falls from the bone. It's one of those dishes where you may not get the timing quite right when you first cook them but you shouldn't give up. The next time, leave them in longer or, if they have cooked too quickly, take them out sooner. You'll get to know.

FOR 4–6

2.5kg ribs (I prefer pork but a lot of people like beef; the choice is yours)
300ml water or stock

For the marinade
150ml soy sauce
150ml cider vinegar or malt vinegar
1 tablespoon ground cinnamon
2 tablespoons dried mixed herbs
1 teaspoon ground black pepper
1 teaspoon salt
2 tablespoons Momma's Cajun Seasoning (page 50)
1 tablespoon ground cumin
15g dried chilli flakes
300g soft dark brown sugar
150ml vegetable oil

For the barbecue sauce
2 x 400g cans of chopped tomatoes
1 orange, peeled and cut into large pieces
1 small can of chopped pineapple
1 onion, roughly chopped
1 red, 1 green and 1 yellow pepper, roughly chopped
250ml distilled white vinegar or cider vinegar
200g soft brown sugar
a pinch each of salt and pepper
2 tablespoons Momma's Cajun Seasoning (page 50)
2 tablespoons smoked paprika
1 small jar of smoky barbecue-flavoured sauce

(optional, but I find it adds a smoky taste and helps to thicken the sauce)

Place all the marinade ingredients except the sugar and oil in a large pan and bring to the boil. Simmer for 5 minutes, then stir in the sugar. Simmer for 20 minutes, until the mixture has reduced to a fairly thick, dark syrup. Remove from the heat, whisk in the oil and leave to cool.

Wash the ribs and pat them dry. You need to decide if you want to cut them into smaller portions or leave as a rack or half rack. I always cut them by counting 3 bones along, which makes a nice portion size, or you could cut them with 2 bones in, which is ideal for buffets and children's portions. Put them in a dish, pour the marinade over and, if possible, leave them in the fridge to marinate overnight. If you are in a hurry, try to marinate them for at least an hour. Meanwhile, make the barbecue sauce. Combine all the ingredients except the bottled sauce in a pan and bring to the boil, then add the bottled sauce, if using. Simmer over a low heat until the mixture has reduced by half; this can take anything from 30 minutes to an hour. It should be fairly thick but still pourable. Remove from the heat and, when it has cooled down a little so you won't burn yourself, blend with a hand-held electric blender. The sauce can be kept in the fridge for up to 2 weeks.

To cook the ribs, pour off the excess marinade (you can keep this, covered, in the fridge for up to a week – you never know, after cooking one batch of ribs you may be forced by the family to cook up another within days). Heat a ridged griddle pan over a high heat and place the ribs on it to seal them. They should sizzle, and the sugar in the marinade should also make them smoke. (When Brian is cooking his ribs, I sometimes have to remind him that he's not cooking outside back home. He just flashes me that smile of his and says, 'Ah, chef, you know they need the smoke, dat's what makes them good.' I smile back and leave him to it, because when I say his ribs are good, *I mean they are real good*!) Cook for about 2 minutes on each side, then transfer to a baking tray. Take 100ml of the marinade and mix it with the water or stock. Stir together and drizzle it over the ribs, holding back a little. Place in an oven preheated to 160°C/Gas Mark 3 and cook for 1 hour. The ribs will release their own juices but if they begin to dry out, add the reserved diluted marinade.

After an hour, top with the barbecue sauce and turn the heat up to 200°C/Gas Mark 6. Cook for 20–30 minutes, until the meat begins to fall from the bones. Let's imagine it's a hot summer's day, though, and friends have just turned up. Why not take those ribs outside and throw them on to the grill? All you need to do is take them out of the oven after the first hour's cooking, place them on a hot grill and brush some of the barbecue sauce over them. Cook for about 5 minutes, then turn the ribs over and cover the other side with the sauce. Cook for a further 5–10 minutes, or until they are cooked through and the meat is starting to fall from the bone. If you are an experienced barbecue cook, then you could start with the raw marinated ribs. Just don't add the sauce until the ribs are nearly cooked – you'll only burn it away if you put it on too soon.

TURKEY ALWAYS REMINDS ME OF THANKSGIVING AND FUN FAMILY TIMES BACK HOME.

I have stuck to the tradition here in the UK, making sure I gather my friends and family together to give thanks and, of course, to eat until we drop. It's the day when all diets must be put on hold.

THANKSGIVING HAS BEEN MY FAVOURITE HOLIDAY EVER SINCE I WAS A CHILD.

You would have thought that Christmas would be the one to capture my heart – after all, that's when all the pretty lights go up and presents appear under the table.

BUT GIVE ME A DAY SURROUNDED BY LOVING FAMILY AND FRIENDS, NO PRESSURE OF GIFT GIVING AND ALL THE TURKEY YOU CAN POSSIBLY EAT, AND I'M AS HAPPY AS A PIG IN MUCK.

ROAST TURKEY

I maintain that a good, fresh roast turkey, stuffed with vegetables and cornbread, is the only way to go. Many butchers source traditionally reared birds from local farms, and even supermarkets now offer organic or free-range turkeys. Take the time to source a good bird and you won't go wrong.

You have to reserve the giblets, plus the juices from roasting the bird, to make the perfect gravy. Homemade cranberry sauce is also a must. My brother, who lives in Georgia, believes that a Southern-style deep-fried turkey is the way of the future, but I won't be throwing out my oven, no way. Turkey may be slipping off the UK Christmas menu, now that goose, duck and other birds are becoming fashionable again, but somehow I don't think it will ever disappear from the American Thanksgiving tradition. It's part of our history and without it we'd be lost.

FOR 15-20

6.8–7.8kg turkey, with giblets
1 onion, cut in half
4 celery stalks, roughly chopped
115g butter
25g fresh sage, chopped, or 2 teaspoons dried sage
1 tablespoon salt
1 teaspoon ground black pepper
1 quantity of Cornbread Stuffing (page 43)

For the gravy
the giblets from the turkey
1 onion, sliced
2 celery stalks, sliced
1 litre water
65g plain flour
salt and pepper

First remove the giblets, which are usually found in a bag inside the cavity of the bird, and set them aside for making gravy. Wash the bird inside and out with cold water, then pat dry. Place in a roasting tin and put half the onion and celery in the cavity. Gently melt 100g of the butter, then stir in half the sage and the salt and pepper. Leave to cool a little, then pour this mixture over the turkey and massage it into the skin. Finely chop the remaining onion and celery, mix them with the remaining butter and sage and gently slide the mixture under the skin of the breast. Loosely pack the cornbread stuffing into the cavity of the bird. Cover the bird with foil and roast in an oven preheated to 180°C/Gas Mark 4 for 1 hour. Remove the foil so the bird can brown and crisp up nicely and roast for a further $2^1/_2$–$3^1/_2$ hours, basting occasionally with the juices in the roasting tin. The rule of thumb is that a bird this size, when stuffed, should take around 15 minutes per 450g. Insert a roasting thermometer between the inner thigh and the breast; when the bird is done, it should register 82°C. Other indications that the bird is done are if the drumstick can be moved up and down easily and the juices run clear when you pierce the flesh with a skewer.

While the bird is roasting, start preparing the stock for the gravy. Place the giblets, onion, celery, water and some salt and pepper in a pan and bring to the boil. Simmer for 40 minutes or until the giblets are tender and the meat begins to fall from the neck. Remove from the heat, take out the giblets and cut them up into small pieces, discarding any gristle. Pick as much meat as possible from the neck and set aside.

When the turkey is done, remove from the oven and transfer to a large platter. Leave to rest for half an hour before carving, so that the meat will absorb its own juices and become more succulent. Meanwhile, finish the gravy. Place the roasting tin with all its juices on top of the stove over a low heat and add all the meat from the giblets. When the drippings begin to bubble, stir in the flour to make a roux. Cook for a few minutes over a low heat, then slowly pour in the hot giblet stock, stirring all the time. Continue to stir until it begins to boil and thicken, then season with salt and pepper to taste. I like a hearty gravy with all the bits in it, although some people prefer to strain it. Carve the turkey and serve with the gravy, plus mashed potatoes, greens, Candied Sweet Potatoes (page 123), Cornbread (page 42) and Cranberry Sauce (page 49).

VEGETABLES & SIDES

BLACK-EYED PEAS WITH HAM
HOPPIN' JOHN
BLACK-EYED PEAS À LA SHACK
VEGETABLE JAMBALAYA
OKRA WITH STEWED TOMATOES
SOUTHERN-STYLE OKRA GUMBO
SPRING GREENS AND KALE WITH HAM HOCKS
SWEET POTATO AND BUTTERNUT SQUASH STEW
PEPPERS STUFFED WITH CORNBREAD
BEEF TOMATOES STUFFED WITH MINCE & MIXED RICE
PEPPERS STUFFED WITH MINCE AND CHORIZO
STUFFED AUBERGINES
BAKED STUFFED SWEET POTATOES

GREEN BEAN VINAIGRETTE
MOMMA'S SOULATOUILLE
ROAST CURRIED BUTTERNUT SQUASH OR PUMPKIN
CANDIED SWEET POTATOES
CANDIED CARROTS
CANDIED BUTTERNUT SQUASH
MACARONI AND CHEESE
FRIED PLANTAIN
CAJUN POTATO WEDGES
STEAMED WHITE CABBAGE AND BUTTER
CABBAGE WITH GAMMON AND PINEAPPLE
SUCCOTASH (THE EASY WAY)
CORN PUDDING
BARBECUE BAKED BEANS
SPICY RED BEANS

BLACK-EYED PEAS WITH HAM

Sometimes known as 'cowboy's caviar', black-eyed peas are as common as baked beans in many homes in the South. Unlike many dried beans, they don't need to be soaked overnight before cooking. I like them cooked with a nice piece of ham or bacon but they are just as good served up as a vegetarian meal or combined with rice, when they are known as Hoppin' John (page 103).

FOR 4–6

300g dried black-eyed peas or 2 x 400g cans of
   black-eyed peas, drained
2 tablespoons vegetable oil
1 onion, diced
1 garlic clove, chopped
1 small green and 1 small red pepper, diced
250g cooked ham or 12 smoked bacon rashers,
   chopped
$1/2$ teaspoon salt
$1/4$ teaspoon pepper
1 teaspoon Momma's Cajun Seasoning (page 50)
2 large tomatoes, chopped, or a 200g can of
   chopped tomatoes
a small bunch of fresh coriander, chopped

If you are using dried black-eyed peas, put them in a large pan with enough water to cover generously and bring to the boil with a little salt. Simmer for 40–50 minutes, until tender but not mushy, then drain well.

Heat the oil in a large frying pan, add the onion, garlic, peppers and ham or bacon and cook for 5 minutes over a medium heat, until the vegetables are softened. Add the cooked black-eyed peas and the salt, pepper and Cajun seasoning and stir together. Continue to cook over a low heat for 10 minutes, then add the tomatoes. Cover and simmer for 15 minutes, then scatter over the coriander.

HOPPIN' JOHN

'Rice and peas' is familiar to anyone from the Caribbean. Well, Hoppin' John is pretty much the same thing. The main difference is that in the Southern states of America, we use black-eyed peas. There are many stories about the origins of the name. I like to believe the one reported by Raymond Sokolov, former food editor of *The New York Times*. He wrote that the dish goes back as far as 1841, when, according to oral tradition, it was sold on the streets of Charleston, South Carolina, by a crippled black man known as Hoppin' John.

Hoppin' John is traditionally served on New Year's Day with cornbread and greens. The black-eyed peas stand for coins, the greens for dollar bills and the cornbread for gold. With all that symbolic money on the table, the hope is that the wealth will continue throughout the year.

FOR 4–6

150g dried black-eyed peas or a 400g can of black-eyed peas, drained
40ml vegetable oil
1 onion, chopped
450g easy-cook American-style rice
1 teaspoon salt
$1/2$ teaspoon pepper
1 teaspoon ground turmeric
1 litre water

If you are using dried black-eyed peas, put them in a large pan with enough water to cover generously and bring to the boil with a little salt. Simmer for 40–50 minutes, until tender but not mushy, then drain well.

Heat the oil in a large pan, add the onion and black-eyed peas and fry until the onion is soft and translucent. Add the rice, salt, pepper and turmeric and stir for about a minute, until the rice is coated with the seasoning and appears translucent. Add the water to the pan and bring to the boil. Reduce the heat a little and cook, uncovered, for about 15 minutes. Try not to disturb the mixture too much. Once the water has all been absorbed and the rice is tender, the dish is ready. Gently fork through the rice, making sure the black-eyed peas are evenly distributed, then serve.

'RICE AND PEAS' IS FAMILIAR TO ANYONE FROM THE CARIBBEAN. WELL, HOPPIN' JOHN IS PRETTY MUCH THE SAME THING.

BLACK-EYED PEAS À LA SHACK

Once again, black-eyed peas are on the menu. I created this recipe while still at the Soul Food Shack. It is a simple meal, which takes just 15 minutes to prepare if you use canned black-eyed peas.

FOR 2–4

4 tablespoons vegetable oil
1 onion, diced
$1/2$ each green, red, and yellow pepper, diced
1 garlic clove, chopped
1 courgette, diced
1 teaspoon Momma's Cajun Seasoning (page 50), or to taste
$1/2$ teaspoon dried chilli flakes, or to taste
400g can of chopped tomatoes
400g can of sweetcorn, drained
400g can of black-eyed peas, drained
200g Cheddar cheese, grated
25g fresh coriander (stalks and leaves), chopped
salt and pepper

Heat the oil in a casserole, add the onion, peppers, garlic and courgette and fry over a medium heat for 5 minutes, until softened. Stir in the Cajun seasoning and chilli flakes, cook for 1 minute more, then pour in the tomatoes. Add the sweetcorn and black-eyed peas and gently fold them into the tomato base. Continue to cook for about 5 minutes, until the sauce has reduced by half but not completely evaporated. Season with salt and pepper. Sprinkle the grated cheese on top and place in a hot oven or under a hot grill for 2 minutes to melt the cheese. Scatter with the coriander. Serve over a bed of rice, with chicken or fish, or on a piece of toast as a quick snack.

VEGETABLE JAMBALAYA

This dish is very similar to the meat version on page 76 except, of course, there is no meat in it. I like to jazz it up by using a mixture of brown, white and wild rice.

FOR 6-8

3 tablespoons vegetable or olive oil

2 onions, 1 roughly chopped, 1 thinly sliced

1 red, 1 green and 1 yellow pepper, half of each diced and the other half cut into strips

1 teaspoon crushed garlic

2 tablespoons Momma's Cajun Seasoning (page 50)

1 tablespoon ground cumin

1 teaspoon cumin seeds (optional but it adds a nice touch if you have them)

1 teaspoon salt

$\frac{1}{2}$ teaspoon ground black pepper

6 vegetarian sausages, sliced

1 chilli, preferably Scotch bonnet, seeded and finely chopped, or left whole

120g wild rice

120g brown rice

120g easy-cook American-style rice

900g mixed vegetables, e.g. 2 carrots, diced, 2 courgettes, diced, 2 handfuls of peas, 2 handfuls of green beans and 3–4 broccoli and cauliflower florets (or use whatever vegetables you have in)

1 litre water or vegetable stock

1 teaspoon gumbo filé (if you have it)

100g smoked tofu, diced

a handful of mushrooms, sliced

Place a large saucepan over a medium heat and add 1 tablespoon of the oil, followed by the one chopped onion, diced pepper halves and crushed garlic. Stir in half the Cajun seasoning and cumin, plus the salt and pepper, then add the vegetarian sausages. Cook for about 5 minutes, until the onion and peppers have softened and the sausages begin to brown. The spices will start to give off their fragrance and coat the pan, which will enhance the dish. I call this seasoning the pot. Now stir in the chopped fresh chilli. Remember that Scotch bonnet chillies are very hot – if you are worried about the heat level, leave the chilli whole and add it to the dish with the water or stock, removing it after 10 minutes. Its wonderful and unique flavour will be released but the heat will be kept to a gentle minimum.

Add the wild, brown and easy-cook rice and stir well, then add the remaining half of the seasoning spices. Stir everything together until the rice is fully coated, then add the mixed vegetables and the water or vegetable stock. Bring to a simmer and add the gumbo filé, if using. Simmer, uncovered, over a low heat for 20 minutes. When the rice has swollen and is almost cooked, add the smoked tofu and simmer for a further 10 minutes. Adjust the seasoning according to taste – you might want to add a touch more chilli.

Heat the remaining 2 tablespoons of oil in a large frying pan, add the one thinly sliced onion, the strips of peppers and the mushrooms and stir-fry for 3 minutes, until tender. Place on top of the jambalaya and serve immediately.

SPRING GREENS AND KALE WITH HAM HOCKS

Greens have always been part of a soul diet, and a Southern one in general. In America a variety can be found. Some, such as turnip greens, are the tops of well-known root vegetables. Other popular varieties, such as collard greens and mustard greens, are closely associated with curly kale and leafy cabbage. When I arrived in the UK, it was a struggle to find greens to prepare for my Sunday meal. Like my slave forefathers, I quickly adapted to what was available, and discovered that by combining spring greens and curly kale I could get very close to the flavours of back home.

This dish is great with or without meat. As I cook for both meat eaters and vegetarians, I usually divide the batch of greens and set aside a small amount for cooking without the meat.

FOR 4–6

750g spring greens
750g curly kale (or green cabbage)
1kg smoked ham hock on the bone (or 500g smoked bacon, chopped)
2 onions, thinly sliced
1 green pepper, thinly sliced
1 garlic clove, finely chopped
1–2 teaspoons dried chilli flakes, depending on how spicy you want it
1 teaspoon salt
1 teaspoon black pepper
2 tablespoons cider vinegar (optional)

Wash and trim the greens – even if I buy them in a packet that says 'washed and trimmed', I tend to give them another wash; good greens always seem to have a bit of mud and sand stuck to them. Chop them roughly and set aside.

If using a ham hock, slice it through to the bone in several places so that it cooks more quickly. Place the ham hock or bacon in a very large pan, add enough water to cover and bring to the boil. Simmer for 30 minutes, then add the onions, green pepper, garlic and chilli flakes and simmer for a further 15 minutes. Check to see that the ham hock is cooked; if not, remove it from the pot, cut the meat from the bone into smaller pieces and return to the pot. This will speed up the cooking. Add the chopped mixed greens, plus the salt and pepper, and give everything a good stir to combine the flavours. You may need to cover the pan with a lid at this stage to help the greens begin to wilt. Depending on your personal preference, you can cook the greens for 10–15 minutes, until just tender, or you can do it the old-fashioned way and cook for 30–45 minutes. They will reduce in volume by at least half.

Remove from the pan, place in a large serving bowl and drizzle the cider vinegar over the top, if using. Serve with any main course.

OKRA WITH STEWED TOMATOES

From the same family as the hibiscus and the cotton plant, okra was brought to America over three centuries ago by African slaves. It's an acquired taste, and one that most people either love or hate. When buying okra, look for young, unblemished pods, tender but not soft, and no more than 10cm long. It can be wrapped in kitchen paper and stored in the refrigerator for 2–3 days, or you can freeze it for up to a year if you blanch it whole for 2 minutes first. When cut, okra releases a sticky substance with thickening properties, which makes it particularly suitable for soups, stews and gumbos. Okra goes well with onions, peppers, and aubergines.

FOR 6-8

1kg fresh (or frozen) okra
100ml vegetable oil
1 onion, chopped
1 garlic clove, chopped
$\frac{1}{2}$ Scotch bonnet chilli, seeded and chopped, or 1
   teaspoon dried chilli flakes
1 teaspoon ground cumin
1 tablespoon Momma's Cajun Seasoning (page 50)
500g tomatoes, roughly chopped, or 2 x 400g cans
   of tomatoes, drained
1 teaspoon salt
$\frac{1}{2}$ teaspoon pepper
25g fresh coriander (stems and leaves), chopped

If you are using fresh okra, trim the ends, then either leave it whole or slice it in half. Heat the vegetable oil in a pan, add the onion, garlic, chilli, cumin and Cajun seasoning and cook over a medium heat until the onion is coated with the seasoning. Stir in the okra and cook for 2–3 minutes to coat. Add the tomatoes, salt and pepper and a splash of water to lubricate. Cover, reduce the heat and cook gently for 15 minutes or until the okra is soft and the tomatoes begin to take on some colour. Sprinkle with the coriander and serve on a bed of rice.

SOUTHERN-STYLE OKRA GUMBO

A variation of the recipe opposite, this full-on soul favourite includes sweetcorn and broad beans to create a hearty gumbo. I tend to cook most vegetables with a little meat but if you want a vegetarian gumbo, simply omit the bacon.

FOR 6-8

2 tablespoons vegetable oil
500g smoked back or streaky bacon rashers, chopped
1 large onion, diced
1 large green pepper, diced
1 garlic clove, diced
1 teaspoon Momma's Cajun Seasoning (page 50)
1 teaspoon dried chilli flakes (optional)
700g fresh (or frozen) okra, cut into 2.5cm pieces
325g fresh or frozen broad beans
2 x 400g cans of plum tomatoes
3 tablespoons tomato purée
450ml vegetable stock (or water)
325g can of sweetcorn, drained
2 tablespoons caster sugar
1 teaspoon gumbo filé
1 teaspoon salt
$1/2$ teaspoon pepper

Heat the oil in a large pan and add the bacon, onion, green pepper, garlic, Cajun seasoning and chilli flakes, if using. Fry gently for 5 minutes, until softened. Add the okra, broad beans, tomatoes, tomato purée and stock and simmer over a low heat for 45 minutes, giving the mixture a stir from time to time to prevent sticking. Stir in the sweetcorn, sugar and gumbo filé and cook for 10 minutes. Season with the salt and pepper, then serve with rice.

SWEET POTATO AND BUTTERNUT SQUASH STEW

This is one of those quick and easy winter stews that are very satisfying when the days begin to shorten. You could purée it, rather than leave it chunky, and serve as a thick soup.

FOR 6

2 tablespoons olive or vegetable oil
1 onion, diced
1 garlic clove, finely chopped
a pinch of ground ginger
1 teaspoon ground cumin
1 teaspoon Momma's Cajun Seasoning (page 50)
$1/2$ small butternut squash (or pumpkin), peeled, seeded and diced
2 orange-fleshed sweet potatoes, peeled and diced
1 white-fleshed sweet potato, peeled and diced
1 potato, peeled and diced
2 carrots, peeled and diced
2 tablespoons soft brown sugar
150g red lentils
100g fresh coriander, chopped
125ml double cream or crème fraîche (optional)
salt and pepper
Sweet Potato Crisps (page 41) or croûtons, to garnish (optional)

Heat the oil in a large pan, add the onion, garlic, ginger, cumin and Cajun seasoning and cook gently until the onion has softened. Stir in the diced squash, potatoes and carrots, then add enough water to cover the vegetables by 2–3cm. Bring to the boil and simmer until the vegetables are soft. Stir in the brown sugar and reduce the heat. If the vegetables have absorbed a lot of the liquid, add enough water just to cover again. Season with salt and pepper, add the lentils and simmer until they are tender. Give the soup a good stir, then add the fresh coriander and remove from the heat. (If you want to serve it as a soup, purée it with a hand blender at this stage.)

To serve, dollop the cream on top, if using, and sprinkle over some freshly fried Sweet Potato Crisps or croûtons, if liked.

PEPPERS STUFFED WITH CORNBREAD

Cornbread stuffing can be used for poultry, fish or vegetables. Stuffed peppers make a great vegetarian main course and also a good accompaniment to meat.

FOR 6

2 red peppers
2 green peppers
2 yellow peppers
6 knobs of butter
1 quantity of Cornbread Stuffing (page 43)
4 tablespoons olive oil
Momma's Cajun Seasoning (page 50), to taste

Scoop out and discard the seeds from the peppers, then put a knob of butter inside each one. Using a tablespoon, fill the peppers with the cornbread stuffing and place in an ovenproof dish. Drizzle with the olive oil, shake some Cajun seasoning on top and place in an oven preheated to 180°C/Gas Mark 4. Bake for 30–40 minutes, until the peppers are tender and the stuffing is heated through.

BEEF TOMATOES STUFFED WITH MINCE & MIXED RICE

This dish looks as though you have spent a lot of time on it, when in reality it is quick and easy to prepare. If you are able to get the big, plump beef tomatoes, try experimenting by stuffing them with a variety of finely chopped meats or vegetables.

FOR 4

4 large beef tomatoes
1 tablespoon vegetable oil
350g minced beef
1 small onion, diced
1 green pepper, diced
1 garlic clove, finely chopped
1 tablespoon Momma's Cajun Seasoning (page 50)
$\frac{1}{2}$–1 teaspoon dried chilli flakes, to taste
120g mixed rice, cooked according to the packet instructions

Carefully slice the top off each tomato and, with a small paring knife, cut around the inside to loosen the pulp. Remove the pulp, chop roughly and set aside.

Heat the vegetable oil in a frying pan, add the mince and onion and fry until the meat has browned. Add the green pepper and garlic and sauté for 3 minutes. Add the Cajun seasoning and chilli flakes and cook for 5 minutes. Pour off any excess oil. Stir in the cooked rice and the chopped tomato pulp. Stuff the tomatoes with the mixture and place in an oven preheated to 180°C/Gas Mark 4. Cook for 50–60 minutes, until the tomatoes are tender and the filling is heated through.

PEPPERS STUFFED WITH MINCE AND CHORIZO

Peppers can be stuffed with a variety of meats, rice, pasta, vegetables and pulses. This is one of my favourite stuffings.

FOR 4

4 large peppers (preferably red, green, yellow and
  orange)
1 tablespoon vegetable oil
400g lean minced beef
1 teaspoon Momma's Cajun Seasoning (page 50)
1 teaspoon ground cumin
1 onion, finely diced
2 chorizo sausages, diced
1 can of cream of mushroom soup
120g rice, cooked according to the packet

instructions
1 tablespoon olive oil

Slice the top off each pepper and scoop out the seeds. Heat the vegetable oil in a frying pan, add the mince and cook for about 5 minutes, until browned. Add the Cajun seasoning, cumin, onion and chorizo and cook for about 5 minutes, until the mince is done. Stir in the cream of mushroom soup and the cooked rice. Remove from the heat and spoon the mixture into the peppers, then drizzle the olive oil on top. Place in an oven preheated to 180°C/Gas Mark 4 and bake for 35–40 minutes, until the peppers are tender and the stuffing is heated through.

STUFFED AUBERGINES

I have served stuffed aubergines in the restaurant since it first opened and they are very popular. Serve as a main course or a substantial side dish.

FOR 4

2 aubergines
2 teaspoons sea salt
1 teaspoon Momma's Cajun Seasoning (page 50)
200ml olive oil
1 onion, diced
1 garlic clove, finely chopped
100g mushrooms, sliced
1 teaspoon dried chilli flakes
$^1/_2$ quantity of Cornbread Stuffing (page 43)

Cut the aubergines lengthways in half and, with a sharp paring knife, carefully scoop out the flesh and set aside. Sprinkle the shells with the sea salt, place them upside-down in a bowl and leave for 20 minutes. Pat dry with kitchen towel, then place the empty aubergine shells in a baking dish, sprinkle with the Cajun seasoning and set aside.

Heat half the olive oil in a frying pan and add the onion, garlic, mushrooms, chilli flakes and scooped-out aubergine flesh. Fry for 5 minutes over a medium heat until all the vegetables are translucent, then stir in the cornbread stuffing. If the mixture is too dry, add a few drops of water. Using a large spoon, fill the empty aubergine shells with the mixture, then drizzle the remaining olive oil on top. Place in an oven preheated to 180°C/Gas Mark 4 and bake for 40–45 minutes, until the stuffing is firm.

BAKED STUFFED SWEET POTATOES

Just like traditional white potatoes, the sweet potato is a versatile vegetable, delicious boiled, baked or fried. This recipe makes a lovely vegetarian main course and can also be served as a side dish with meat.

FOR 6

3 large sweet potatoes
1 tablespoon olive oil
1 small onion, finely diced
1small green pepper, finely diced
1 red pepper, finely diced
2 celery stalks, finely diced
1 red chilli, finely diced
50g coriander (leaves and stalks), chopped
60g butter
100ml single or double cream (depending on how rich you want it to be)
1 tablespoon Momma's Cajun Seasoning (page 50)

1 teaspoon salt
$1/_2$ teaspoon black pepper

Wash and dry the sweet potatoes, then slice them in half lengthways and rub them all over with the olive oil. Place on the top shelf of an oven preheated to 180°C/Gas Mark 4 and bake for 45–50 minutes, until the flesh is soft. Remove from the oven and leave until cool enough to handle. Using a tablespoon, scoop out the flesh into a bowl, being careful not to split the skin. Put the empty shells on a baking sheet and set aside.

Add all the remaining ingredients to the potato flesh and mix well. Spoon the mixture into the sweet potato shells and return to the oven. Bake for 20–25 minutes, until they are thoroughly heated through and a thin crust has formed on top.

GREEN BEAN VINAIGRETTE

This makes a pleasant change from salad. It is designed to be served and eaten warm, as a side dish, but if it cools down it doesn't matter, as it will still taste good.

FOR 4-6

500g green beans
100ml olive oil
100g spring onions, chopped
1 teaspoon sea salt
1 teaspoon English mustard powder

1 tablespoon red wine vinegar
25g fresh coriander (stalks and leaves), chopped
juice of 1 lemon

Place the green beans in a pan of salted water and bring to the boil. Simmer for 5 minutes, until the beans are tender but not overcooked. Drain well. Put the oil, spring onions, salt, mustard, vinegar, chopped coriander and lemon juice in a bowl and mix well. Place the warm green beans in a serving dish, pour the vinaigrette over and gently toss together.

MOMMA'S SOULATOUILLE

I created this recipe while cooking for the crowds up in Scotland at the 2006 Edinburgh Fringe Festival. It is based on an old Bajan (that's short for Barbadian) dish, with a touch of French and American soul thrown in. So it might remind you of a dish from the Caribbean or an old-fashioned Provençal ratatouille, thus inspiring the name, 'soulatouille'. You can give your own spin to this dish by adding more vegetables, if you like.

FOR 4–6

1 large aubergine, cut into cubes
1 tablespoon sea salt
1 large onion, roughly diced
1 red and 1 green pepper, roughly diced
olive or vegetable oil for frying
1 tablespoon cumin seeds
1 teaspoon dried chilli flakes, or $\frac{1}{2}$ Scotch bonnet chilli, seeded and finely chopped
2 tablespoons Momma's Cajun Seasoning (page 50)
1 garlic clove, finely chopped
1 small knob of fresh ginger, peeled and finely chopped
500g fresh (or frozen) okra, trimmed and sliced lengthways in half
1 large potato, peeled and diced
400g can of chopped tomatoes
1 tablespoon tomato purée
a little water or vegetable stock, if needed
a heart full of love and soul

Spread the aubergine cubes out on some kitchen paper, sprinkle with the sea salt and leave while you prepare the rest of the ingredients. This will help to release some of the juices and remove the bitterness often associated with aubergine. By the time you have finished cutting all the rest of the vegetables, the aubergine will be ready. Try to cut the onion and peppers about the same size as the aubergine cubes – all should be chunky.

Pour enough oil into a large pan to cover the base and place over a medium heat. Add the diced onion, peppers, cumin seeds, chilli, Cajun seasoning, garlic and ginger and cook until the onion has softened; you should be able to smell the ginger. Add the aubergine, okra and potato and give everything a good stir, making sure all the vegetables are coated with the seasonings. Cook for about 2–3 minutes, until the aubergine begins to reduce in size and release its natural juices. Add the tomatoes and tomato purée. At this stage you can add a little water or vegetable stock if you want a wetter version, although the longer you cook the dish the more juices will be released from the vegetables. Continue to stir and, while stirring, add your own love and soul to the pot. Cover and simmer for about 30 minutes, until all the vegetables are tender, stirring frequently so the tomatoes don't stick to the bottom of the pan. Serve over a bed of Hoppin' John (page 103), with Jerk Chicken (page 92) or other meat.

ROAST CURRIED BUTTERNUT SQUASH OR PUMPKIN

This dish can be varied by adding or substituting root vegetables such as carrots, swede or turnips – or try courgettes or whatever takes your fancy. After removing the seeds from the squash, you could roast them for a healthy snack. Let them dry out, then put them on a lightly greased baking tray, sprinkle with sea salt and place in a hot oven. The roasting time will depend on how wet the seeds are – anything from 15–45 minutes, but be careful not to burn them.

FOR 4–6

1 butternut squash or pumpkin, peeled, seeded and
   cut into small cubes
2 large onions, roughly chopped
1 teaspoon sea salt
2 tablespoons mild curry powder
1 teaspoon dried chilli flakes
1 tablespoon cumin seeds
100g soft brown sugar
70ml olive oil
soured cream, crème fraîche or yoghurt, to serve

Place the squash or pumpkin and onions in a roasting tin and sprinkle the salt, curry powder, chilli flakes, cumin seeds, brown sugar and olive oil over the top. Using your hands, gently massage the seasonings into the vegetables, then leave to stand for about 15 minutes so that the flavours begin to be absorbed. Place on the top shelf of an oven preheated to 180°C/Gas Mark 4 and bake for 35–40 minutes, until the vegetables are tender. Serve with soured cream, crème fraîche or yoghurt.

ROAST VEGETABLE TRIO

Use potatoes, sweet potatoes and pumpkin. Cut them into wedges, with their skins on, and parboil them. Drain well and place on a baking tray. Sprinkle with sea salt and Cajun seasoning, then drizzle with olive oil and rub it in to coat the vegetables thoroughly. Bake on the top shelf of an oven preheated to 180°C/Gas Mark 4 for 25–30 minutes, until the vegetables and their skins begin to crisp up.

AN ODE TO THE ALMIGHTY SWEET POTATO

SWEET POTATOES ARE ONE OF THE MOST VERSATILE SOUL FOOD VEGETABLES AROUND.

You will find them on all holiday tables – boiled, mashed, candied and topped with marshmallows, or even made into pies and puddings for dessert.

The sweet potato is surprisingly healthy. Rich in vitamin E, it is virtually fat free and contains just 118 calories per medium potato. It can be traced back to the time of slavery, when it was cultivated by our forefathers in the Southern states of America. George Washington Carver (1864–1943), a black scientist renowned for his research into the peanut, developed 118 by-products of sweet potatoes in order to help Southern farmers utilise their crops to the full. (He also developed over 300 uses for peanuts, including peanut butter, every small American child's favourite.)

MANY PEOPLE BACK HOME CALL SWEET POTATOES 'YAMS'.

The terms are used interchangeably but in fact they are two entirely different vegetables. The yam is the tuber of a tropical vine and is not even distantly related to the sweet potato.

CANDIED SWEET POTATOES

Candied sweet potatoes topped with marshmallows are another holiday soul favourite. I have cooked this dish every Thanksgiving and Christmas for the past 40 years. It was one of the first holiday dishes shown to me by my grandmother, mother and aunts. You always knew there was some serious cooking going on when their sweet aroma wafted through the house. I cooked the dish on BBC television for Thanksgiving 2005, with Antony Worrall Thompson and Gary Rhodes. Gary was a bit shocked when the marshmallows came out but I explained that we Americans like to combine sweet and savoury tastes. He stepped forward with his fork, took a big mouthful and declared it 'delicious'.

FOR 4–6

4 medium-sized sweet potatoes (a mixture of orange- and white-fleshed ones, if you like)
110g butter
100g soft dark brown sugar
1 teaspoon ground cinnamon
1 teaspoon vanilla extract
1 orange
marshmallows for topping

Place the unpeeled sweet potatoes in a large pot of water. Bring to the boil, then reduce the heat and simmer until they are soft but not falling apart. Remove from the water and peel. Either slice them into 2.5cm-thick pieces, chop into cubes or mash them – it doesn't matter. Arrange in a casserole or on a baking tray and set aside.

Put the butter and brown sugar in a pan and heat gently, stirring until melted. Stir in the cinnamon and vanilla. Cut the orange in half and squeeze the juice into the mixture. I also like to grate a bit of the zest into the sauce. Simmer for a couple of minutes, until the sauce begins to thicken, then remove from the heat and pour it over the sweet potatoes. It may seem like a lot of sauce but the dish is meant to be rich and juicy. Place in an oven preheated to 180°C/Gas Mark 4 and bake for 15–20 minutes, until the sauce has begun to bubble and thicken at the sides. Remove and top with the marshmallows. Return to the oven and continue to cook for about 5 minutes, until the marshmallows are golden and have melted. Serve hot, with chicken, turkey or Meatloaf (page 74) and any vegetables you like.

YOU ALWAYS KNEW THERE WAS SOME SERIOUS COOKING GOING ON WHEN THEIR SWEET AROMA WAFTED THROUGH THE HOUSE.

CANDIED CARROTS

Soul food tends to be a combination of sweet and savoury. It's not unusual to find a vegetable smothered in a candied sauce. Some of the dishes originally included sugar to help preserve them, others just out of the desire for something sweet.

When making a candied sauce, don't overcook it or it will harden. This basic candied sauce can be used with a variety of vegetables, fruits and desserts.

FOR 4–6

1kg carrots

For the candied sauce
110g butter
100g soft brown sugar
1 teaspoon ground cinnamon
1 teaspoon vanilla extract
zest and juice of 1 orange

First make the sauce. Melt the butter and sugar in a saucepan, then add the cinnamon, vanilla and orange zest and juice and simmer for 3–5 minutes, until the sugar begins to bubble.

Peel the carrots and cut them to your own preference – diced, sliced or in long strips. Put them in a pan, cover with water and bring to the boil. Simmer until the carrots are tender but not limp. Drain well, place on a baking tray and pour the candied sauce over them. Bake in an oven preheated to 180°C/Gas Mark 4, until the sauce begins to thicken and bubble. Serve with chicken, turkey, roast potatoes and any other vegetable.

CANDIED BUTTERNUT SQUASH

This is a variation on my Candied Carrots. Oddly enough, we tend to candy a lot of orange and yellow vegetables – perhaps capitalising on their natural sweetness.

FOR 4–6

115g butter
100g soft brown sugar
1 teaspoon ground cinnamon
1 teaspoon vanilla extract
zest and juice of 1 orange
1 butternut squash, peeled, seeded and cut into small cubes

To make the sauce, melt the butter and sugar in a saucepan, then add the cinnamon, vanilla and orange zest and juice. Simmer for 3–5 minutes, until the sugar begins to bubble. Place the squash cubes in an ovenproof dish, pour the sauce over the top, then bake in an oven preheated to 180°C/Gas Mark 4 for 30–40 minutes, until the squash is soft and juicy.

MACARONI AND CHEESE

No holiday feast or Sunday dinner is complete without a large helping of Southern-style macaroni and cheese on the side. My mother is famous as the champion mac-cheese maker, although I think I am now taking over the title. She taught me the secret of combining various strong cheeses to make the perfect blend. I feel my recipe tops hers only because over here in England there is a wider variety of farmhouse cheeses and they tend to be stronger. A few of my favourites are suggested below, but the choice is yours. Go out and experiment with an assortment of cheeses; the trick is to ensure you include at least one blue cheese. Once you have made the cheese sauce it will keep in the fridge for 3–5 days, ready for use in a variety of dishes.

FOR 6–8

500g dried macaroni
1 teaspoon olive oil
salt

For the cheese sauce
75g butter
50g plain flour
1 teaspoon salt
1 teaspoon Momma's Cajun Seasoning (page 50)
1 tablespoon mild American mustard (or English mustard if you want an added kick)
1 litre milk
100g Stilton cheese, crumbled
100g mature Red Leicester cheese, grated
150g mature English Cheddar cheese, grated
100g mature Wexford Irish Cheddar cheese, grated

Making a nice cheese sauce takes a little time and patience. You don't want to walk away while it's cooking because it can easily stick and begin to burn, and if it catches, believe me, it's hard to get rid of the taste or disguise it. To start, melt the butter in a medium saucepan over a low heat. Stir in the flour with a wooden spoon and mix until you have a smooth paste (a roux). Stir in the salt, Cajun seasoning and mustard. Continue to cook the roux for at least 1 minute; you need to make sure that the flour is cooked. Slowly add the milk, stirring while you bring it to simmering point. Once you have added all the milk, simmer for at least 5 minutes. When the sauce begins to thicken, stir in the cheeses, reserving half the English Cheddar to use as a topping. Remove from the heat.

Bring a large pan of water to the boil, then add some salt and the olive oil. Add the macaroni to the boiling water and cook according to the directions on the packet, or until the pasta is soft but not mushy and overdone. Drain into a colander and transfer to a casserole or ovenproof dish. Pour the cheese sauce over the pasta and stir it in. Sprinkle the remaining grated cheese on top and bake in an oven preheated to 180°C/Gas Mark 4 for 20 minutes or until the top begins to brown. Whatever you do, do not allow the pasta to dry out. If it's too dry, simply add a little milk to the dish and gently stir it in, being careful not to disturb the crusty top.

VARIATION

Try adding tuna, cooked chicken or any smoked meat or fish. When I was a child, it was the standard Monday-night meal: leftover macaroni and cheese, leftover baked chicken or canned tuna, and whatever vegetables we had. They would all be put into a casserole dish with a little extra milk and grated cheese stirred in. Then, the best bit of all, Mum would sprinkle potato crisps over the top with a little more grated cheese. Into the oven at 180°C/Gas Mark 4 for 15 minutes, and hey presto!, another brilliant meal made from what was to hand.

FRIED PLANTAIN

The plantain is a relative of the banana, but larger and less sweet. It should always be cooked before being eaten. They used to be available only in ethnic markets but nowadays you can often find them in supermarkets, too. Green or unripe plantains are used in soups and stews or served boiled or mashed. As they begin to ripen and turn yellow, the high starch content turns to sugar. This is when I like to cook them – simply peeled, sliced and fried. Fried plantain goes well with Cornbread (page 42) and all sorts of chicken and fish dishes.

FOR 4-6

2 ripe plantains
a knob of butter or a spoonful of vegetable oil

Peel the plantains and slice them thinly. Heat the butter or oil in a frying pan, add the plantain slices and fry gently until golden brown on both sides. Simple and delicious!

NO HOLIDAY FEAST OR SUNDAY DINNER IS COMPLETE WITHOUT A LARGE HELPING OF SOUTHERN-STYLE MACARONI AND CHEESE ON THE SIDE.

CAJUN POTATO WEDGES

This is my alternative to chips. They are so quick and easy to make, and because they use the whole potato there is no waste. Serve as a snack or side dish.

FOR 2-4

4–6 potatoes
vegetable oil for shallow-frying
Momma's Cajun Seasoning (page 50)
sea salt

Wash but don't peel the potatoes and cut each one into 8 wedges. Place in a pan of water, bring to the boil, then reduce the heat and simmer for 10 minutes. Drain and pat dry on kitchen paper.

Heat a good layer of oil in a large frying pan. Add the potatoes and cook until they are soft and slightly blackened, but not burnt. Remove from the frying pan and sprinkle with Cajun seasoning and a touch of sea salt.

STEAMED WHITE CABBAGE AND BUTTER

Cabbage can sometimes be quite dull but, cooked in this simple way, it becomes deliciously sweet and tender.

FOR 4-6

1 medium-sized firm white cabbage
100g butter
1 onion, thinly sliced
1 red pepper, thinly sliced
125ml water
1 teaspoon white sugar
1 teaspoon sea salt
$1/2$ teaspoon cracked black pepper

Cut the cabbage into quarters or sixths, depending on how many people you are serving. Remove any wilted or discoloured leaves and cut out the central core.

Place the butter, onion, red pepper and water in a large pan and bring to the boil. Add the cabbage, sugar, salt and pepper, cover the pan and reduce to a simmer. Cook, stirring occasionally, for 15–20 minutes, until the cabbage is tender. Serve hot with Meatloaf (page 74), chicken or fish and rice.

CABBAGE WITH GAMMON AND PINEAPPLE

This dish is ideal if you are in a hurry and need to throw something together that every member of the family will enjoy. The pineapple makes it a big hit with children.

FOR 4–6

2 tablespoons vegetable oil
1 onion, sliced
1 green pepper, sliced
1 teaspoon dried chilli flakes
$^1/_2$ teaspoon salt
$^1/_4$ teaspoon coarse black pepper
500g gammon joint, cut into 5mm cubes
400g can of pineapple pieces
1 firm white or green cabbage, cored and cut into
   2.5cm pieces

Heat the oil in a large frying pan, add the onion, green pepper, chilli flakes, salt and pepper and fry over a medium heat for 5 minutes, until softened. Add the diced gammon, fry for 5–10 minutes, until browned, then add the pineapple pieces and their juice. Place the cabbage on top and cover the pan with a lid. Simmer for 5–10 minutes, until the cabbage has wilted, then remove the lid and stir. Turn the heat up to cook away some of the liquid. Once the liquid has evaporated and the ham is cooked through, the dish is ready.

SUCCOTASH (THE EASY WAY)

Almost every time a new customer sees succotash on the menu, they're surprised to find it's a real dish rather than just a cartoon expletive – you know, 'Suffering succotash!' Well, I can tell you that it is indeed a real dish, and a very old one at that, going back to the early days when the American settlers and Native American Indians met up for the first Thanksgiving. It's a simple combination of corn and beans. The most commonly used beans are lima beans. When I first came to the UK, I couldn't find lima beans and no one knew what they were, so for nearly 20 years I did without them. Then one day while out shopping I discovered frozen broad beans, which are very similar to lima beans, and my quest to make succotash finally came to an end.

Many recipes use creamed corn but my family didn't, and I like to stick to the recipe I grew up with. You can always add some double cream at the end if you want a creamier version.

FOR 6

65g butter
1 small onion, chopped
1 small red pepper and 1 small green pepper, finely diced
2 x 325g cans of sweetcorn, drained (or about 600g frozen sweetcorn)
350g shelled fresh broad beans (or use frozen broad beans)
250ml water
1 teaspoon cider vinegar or malt vinegar
100ml double cream (optional)
salt and pepper
knob of butter, to serve

Put the butter, onion and peppers in a pan. Add the sweetcorn and beans, then pour in the water, stir well and season with a pinch of salt and pepper. Place over a moderate heat, bring to a simmer and cook gently, uncovered, for about 20 minutes, adding the vinegar at the end. If you are using the cream, this is the time to add it. Simmer for 5 minutes, until the mixture has thickened, then check the seasoning and serve with the knob of butter on top.

ALMOST EVERY TIME A NEW CUSTOMER SEES SUCCOTASH ON THE MENU, THEY'RE SURPRISED TO FIND IT'S A REAL DISH RATHER THAN JUST A CARTOON EXPLETIVE – YOU KNOW, 'SUFFERING SUCCOTASH!'

CORN PUDDING

I know this sounds like dessert, but please believe me when I say it is served with the main course. You will by now be beginning to understand the sweet tooth associated with soul food. We eat corn and rice pudding with our main meals. If raisins and a touch more sugar are added, then it could be served as a dessert.

FOR 8-10

2 x 325g cans of sweetcorn, drained (or use well-drained thawed frozen sweetcorn)
200g caster sugar
4 eggs, beaten

475ml milk
2 tablespoons plain flour or cornflour
1 teaspoon salt
1 teaspoon vanilla extract
30g butter

Put the sweetcorn, sugar, eggs and milk in a bowl and mix until the sugar has dissolved. Add the flour or cornflour, salt and vanilla, then pour into a greased wide casserole dish and dot with the butter. Bake in an oven preheated to 180°C/Gas Mark 4 for 50–60 minutes, until a knife inserted in the centre comes out clean. Serve warm.

BARBECUE BAKED BEANS

Baked beans have always been part of my diet. Growing up poor in the ghetto, we were issued with army surplus baked beans, huge blocks of processed cheese, corned beef, tinned tomatoes, and other foods delivered to low-waged families. To overcome the embarrassment of government-surplus food, the women had to come up with creative ways of disguising it. This recipe and the one for Spicy Red Beans that follows can be created from basic store-cupboard ingredients.

FOR 4

2 cans of baked beans
1 onion, diced

1 green pepper, diced
200g can of pineapple chunks
3 tablespoons soft brown sugar
50g butter
125ml maple syrup
2 teaspoons mild American mustard
6 smoked streaky bacon rashers (optional)

Combine all the ingredients except the bacon in a bowl and mix well. Transfer to a casserole dish and, if you are using the bacon, place the rashers on top. Place in an oven preheated to 180°C/Gas Mark 4 and bake for 45 minutes, until the bacon begins to crisp up and brown and the beans bubble up.

SPICY RED BEANS

Like black-eyed peas, red beans are very popular in soul cooking. Which you use depends on where you come from. My family usually went for black-eyed peas, while my brother's wife, who's from Florida, always opts for red beans. There are many recipes for red beans and rice, which is similar to Hoppin' John (page 103).

FOR 6–8

200g dried kidney beans or 2 x 400g cans of kidney
  beans, drained
40ml vegetable oil
2 onions, diced
1 garlic clove, chopped
1 red and 1 green pepper, diced
$1/2$ Scotch bonnet chilli, seeded and finely diced
a pinch of cayenne pepper
1 ham hock or 8 smoked bacon rashers
2 bay leaves
2 tablespoons Worcestershire sauce
2 tablespoons cider vinegar
2 litres vegetable or meat stock
salt and pepper

If you are using dried kidney beans, you'll need to soak them overnight. The next day, make sure you pour off all the water and rinse the beans twice. Then place them in a large pot and bring to the boil. Skim off any white foam from the surface with a slotted spoon and boil hard for a good 10 minutes (this is important to eliminate toxins). Reduce the heat and simmer for 1 hour or until the beans are tender. Drain and set aside.

Heat the oil in a large pan, add the onions, garlic, peppers, chilli, cayenne and some salt and pepper. Cook over a moderate heat until the onions become translucent. If using a ham hock, cut as much meat as you can away from the bone and chop it into 1cm cubes; if you are using bacon, cut it up small. Turn up the heat, add the meat (and the bone, if using a ham hock) to the pot and cook for about 5 minutes, until the meat is browned all over. Stir in the beans, bay leaves, Worcestershire sauce and vinegar, then pour in the stock. Bring to the boil, give it a good stir and reduce the heat again. Cook over a low heat for at least 1 hour or until the ham hock or bacon is cooked. Serve with rice or any meat dish.

BAKING

SWEET POTATO
PIE WITH PECANS

PECAN PIE

ORANGE AND LEMON
SOURED CREAM CAKE

PEACH COBBLER

ALL-AMERICAN APPLE PIE
WITH A CRANBERRY TWIST

KEY LIME PIE

SOFT CHOCOLATE CHIP COOKIES

SWEET POTATO CUSTARD

POUND CAKE

CHOCOLATE BROWNIES

DAOOD'S APPLE CAKE

PINEAPPLE

UPSIDE-DOWN CAKE

CINNAMON BUNS

SOUTHERN BISCUITS

SWEET POTATO PIE WITH PECANS

This recipe is for two 23cm pies. When making desserts, I often like to do a double portion so I can freeze one. Sweet potato pies keep really well in the freezer.

This is my mother's recipe. Everyone has their own version but this one is particularly straight-forward. If you aren't keen on nuts, just leave them out.

MAKES 2 LARGE PIES OR 24 INDIVIDUAL ONES

1kg sweet potatoes
300g softened butter
300g caster sugar
400ml can of sweetened condensed milk
4 eggs
2 teaspoons ground cinnamon
2 teaspoons grated nutmeg
2 teaspoons vanilla extract
2 teaspoons lemon juice
a handful of pecan nuts (or walnuts) for topping

For the sweet pastry
250g plain flour
$1/2$ teaspoon salt
2 tablespoons caster sugar
130g butter, diced
4 tablespoons cold water

To make the pastry, combine the flour, salt and sugar in a mixing bowl. Using 2 knives in a scissor action, cut the butter into the flour until it has formed coarse crumbs. Add the water a tablespoon at a time, mixing it in with the knives until a dough has formed. With floured hands, pat the dough into a smooth ball and push down to flatten it. Cover with cling film and chill for 30 minutes, Then divide it into 2 balls and roll out each one thinly. Use to line two 23cm tart tins, trim the edges, then pinch them at the top to flute them. Alternatively you could make little mini pies using muffin tins. Cut out small circles of pastry and use to line the tins. Chill until ready to use.

Place the sweet potatoes in their skins in a large pot of water. Bring to the boil, then reduce the heat and simmer until they are soft but not falling apart; a knife should pass through them easily. Remove from the water and gently peel off the skin. Place the flesh in a large bowl and add the softened butter and the sugar. Mix together with an electric mixer or a potato masher until smooth. Add the condensed milk, eggs, cinnamon, nutmeg, vanilla and lemon juice and mix until the mixture is lump free and resembles a smooth mash.

Fill the pastry cases three-quarters full and top with the pecans or walnuts. Place the pies in an oven preheated to 180°C/Gas Mark 4 and bake for about 45 minutes to 1 hour, until the filling is firm and golden brown. Serve either warm or cold, with ice cream. Once the pies are completely cold, you can wrap them tightly and freeze for up to 3 months.

PECAN PIE

When the French settled in New Orleans they discovered the pecan. There quickly followed a flurry of new and exciting recipes: pecan brittle, pecan sauces and, of course, the famous pecan pie.

This version is a quick and simple one. You will notice that I have not pre-baked the pie crust. In America we usually cook the whole pie from scratch. This recipe calls for American corn syrup, which is available in some shops under the brand name, Karo syrup. Golden syrup makes a good substitute. The trick to this pie is to roast the pecans before cooking. This can be done once the oven is hot. Simply spread the pecans out on a baking tray and place in the oven to roast for 5–10 minutes. Remember you are roasting the nuts, not burning them, so be careful not to overdo it.

FOR 8-10

1 quantity of Sweet Pastry (page 136)
200ml corn syrup or golden syrup
200g soft brown sugar
$^1/_4$ teaspoon salt
1 teaspoon vanilla extract
100g butter, melted
3 eggs, lightly beaten
250g pecans nuts, lightly toasted
ice cream, to serve

Roll out the pastry, not too thinly, and use to line a 23cm tart tin. I like to fold the edge over to make a thick crust. Chill for at least an hour.

In a mixing bowl, combine the syrup, brown sugar, salt, vanilla and melted butter. Add the eggs and beat until smooth. Remove the pastry case from the fridge and carefully pour the mixture into it. Sprinkle the pecans on top, pushing some of them under the filling with a spoon. Some will sink to the bottom while others will float on top. Place the pie on the middle shelf of an oven preheated to 180°C/Gas Mark 4 and bake for 20 minutes. Take the pie out and place strips of foil over the pastry edge to protect it from burning. Be careful not to spill the filling, as it will still be a little runny. Return the pie to the oven and cook for a further 20 minutes. It's done when a knife inserted in the centre comes out clean; give it an extra 5–10 minutes, if necessary. Remove from the oven and leave to cool. Serve with an ice cream of your choice – vanilla would go well.

WHEN THE FRENCH SETTLED IN NEW ORLEANS THEY DISCOVERED THE PECAN. THERE QUICKLY FOLLOWED A FLURRY OF NEW AND EXCITING RECIPES: PECAN BRITTLE, PECAN SAUCES AND, OF COURSE, THE FAMOUS PECAN PIE.

MOMMA CHERRI'S SOUL IN A BOWL COOKBOOK

ORANGE AND LEMON SOURED CREAM CAKE

This moist cake is good for parties. The original recipe called for just orange but I like to add lemon to lift the flavour. I have now nicknamed it St Clement's cake!

FOR 8–10

125g butter
1 teaspoon salt
1 tablespoon grated orange zest
1 tablespoon grated lemon zest
200g caster sugar
2 eggs
300g plain flour
1 teaspoon baking powder
250ml soured cream
50ml freshly squeezed orange juice
50ml freshly squeezed lemon juice

For the vanilla icing
340g icing sugar
60g softened unsalted butter
2 tablespoons boiling water
1 teaspoon vanilla extract
grated orange and lemon zest, to decorate

In a large bowl, cream the butter, salt, orange and lemon zest together, then gradually beat in the sugar. Add the eggs, one at a time, beating well after each addition. Sift the flour and baking powder together and fold them into the creamed mixture, alternating with the soured cream and orange and lemon juice. Spoon into two greased 12 x 20cm loaf tins or one 23cm square baking tin and place in an oven preheated to 180°C/Gas Mark 4. Bake for 20–30 minutes for the smaller cakes, 35–40 minutes for the larger one, until a skewer inserted in the centre comes out clean. Remove from the oven and leave to cool.

Meanwhile, make the icing. Sift the icing sugar into a bowl, add the butter and beat until pale and creamy. Slowly mix in the boiling water, stopping when you have a spreadable consistency. Stir in the vanilla extract.

Turn the cake out of the tin and spread the icing over the top. Sprinkle over orange and lemon zest to decorate.

PEACH COBBLER

Americans have many ways of making cobblers, depending on which state they come from. Some have a pastry base, some have a crumble topping or a scone-like topping, while others have both a pastry base and a topping. My version is more of a northern one and is very quick to throw together. It is quite similar to an English crumble, with a topping and no pastry base.

I use canned peaches. You could substitute fresh peaches or any other fruit you like, but you will need to add a small amount of sugar syrup. Canned fruit works well and is much quicker.

FOR 4–6

2 x 400g cans of sliced peaches
100g soft brown sugar
100g butter
1 tablespoon ground cinnamon
1 teaspoon vanilla extract
2 teaspoons arrowroot or cornflour, mixed to a paste
    with 2 teaspoons water
vanilla ice cream or whipped cream, to serve

For the topping
150g self-raising flour
150g caster sugar
a touch of ground cinnamon
2 eggs
150g softened butter

Place the canned peaches and 100ml of their juice in a saucepan with the brown sugar, butter, cinnamon and vanilla. Heat gently until the sugar and butter have melted, then stir in the arrowroot or cornflour paste. Cook over a moderate heat for 5–8 minutes, until the mixture begins to thicken; don't let it boil, just keep it on a gentle simmer.

Meanwhile, make the topping. Mix the flour, sugar and cinnamon together in a bowl. Add the eggs and butter and mix well with a wooden spoon (or, if you want to do it my way, with your hands) until the mixture is soft and crumbly; it should not be too wet. Pour the fruit mixture into an ovenproof dish and drop spoonfuls of the topping on to it. Place in an oven preheated to 180°C/Gas Mark 4 and bake for 25–30 minutes, until the topping is golden brown and the edges begin to bubble. Serve either hot or cold, with vanilla ice cream and/or whipped cream.

ALL-AMERICAN APPLE PIE WITH A CRANBERRY TWIST

The pastry I use here is a greatly simplified version of an American flaky cream cheese pie crust. The original recipe is long and involves far too many steps. My view is that if you want to bake a pie, you don't want to have to wait hours for the pastry 'to be right'.

FOR 6-8

4 large cooking apples
3 eating apples
115g butter
75g soft brown sugar
75g caster sugar
1 tablespoon cornflour
1 teaspoon ground cinnamon
$1/4$ teaspoon freshly grated nutmeg
1 teaspoon vanilla extract
115g dried cranberries

For the cream cheese pastry
350g plain flour
50g caster sugar
100g softened butter
125g cream cheese
a pinch of salt
a pinch of baking powder
$1/2$ teaspoon ground cinnamon
about 2 tablespoons ice-cold water
a little milk for brushing

Let's start with the pastry. Simply combine all the ingredients except the milk in a bowl, using a fork to mix well, ending with a small amount of ice-cold water to bind it all together. Place the dough in a plastic bag and knead gently for about 3 minutes, but don't overwork it – remember it is meant to be quick and simple. Place the bag in the fridge for about 30 minutes while you get on with the filling.

This is real easy and quick to prepare. Simply peel and core all the apples, then cut them into slices about 2cm thick, keeping the cookers and eaters separate. Put the cooking apples in a large bowl with 100g of the butter, plus the sugars, cornflour, spices and vanilla. Place in a microwave for about 2 minutes to soften the mixture and release the juices from the apples (or you can do this on top of the stove in a saucepan). Stir in the dessert apples and dried cranberries and set aside.

Remove the pastry from the fridge and divide it into 2 pieces, one slightly larger than the other. Lightly roll out the larger piece on a floured work surface and use it to line a 23cm pie plate. Roll out the remaining piece for the top. The pastry is quite soft but if it breaks, don't worry, you can simply piece it together. Gently spoon the apples into the lined pie plate. Cut up the reserved butter and dot it on the top, then cover with the remaining pastry. Using a fork, gently press all along the edges to seal the pastry, then prick the top a few times to allow it to breathe. If you want a prettier look, you could make a lattice pattern of strips across the top of the pie instead. To give it a good brown colour, brush it with a little milk. Place in an oven preheated to 190°C/Gas Mark 5 and bake for 30–35 minutes, until the pastry is golden brown. The apples have already been softened, so they don't need a long time to finish cooking. I recommend placing a baking tray under the pie in case the juices overflow.

Allow to cool a little, then serve warm, with ice cream, custard or whipped cream – or if you want to go all out, have all 3 toppings.

KEY LIME PIE

Key lime pie originated in the Florida Keys in the 1800s, when fresh ingredients other than local limes were hard to find. Key limes are also referred to as Mexican limes. They are small, with a thin, greenish-yellow skin, and hold a lot of juice. I have found them in markets in the UK but any fresh limes will do.

This recipe uses ginger biscuits for the base, which make an ideal combination with lime. It was given to me by one of my regular customers, who we all refer to as 'Key Lime Kelly'. From start to finish, the pie takes just 20 minutes, so it is a great dish to make if you are in a hurry.

FOR 6-8

250g ginger nut biscuits
125g butter, melted
400ml can of sweetened condensed milk
2 eggs
125ml freshly squeezed lime juice (about 6–10 limes)
juice of 1 lemon
grated zest of 2 limes
ice cream or whipped cream, to serve
slices of lime, to garnish

Crush the biscuits by putting them in a plastic bag and pounding with a rolling pin until powdery. Transfer them to a bowl and add the melted butter. Stir well, then place in the base of a 23cm pie tin and pat into place.

Put the condensed milk and eggs in a bowl and stir with a fork, gradually adding the lime and lemon juice. The mixture will begin to thicken. Add half the lime zest and pour the mixture on top of the ginger crust. Sprinkle the remaining zest on top. Place in an oven preheated to 180°C/Gas Mark 4 and cook for 10 minutes only. Don't be fooled by the look of the pie into thinking you need to cook it for longer. It is meant to be custard-like. It is not a baked cheesecake, although it does look and taste a bit like one. Once cooled, place in the fridge where it will continue to set. Serve with ice cream or whipped cream.

THIS RECIPE WAS GIVEN TO ME BY ONE OF MY REGULAR CUSTOMERS, WHO WE ALL REFER TO AS 'KEY LIME KELLY'.

SOFT CHOCOLATE CHIP COOKIES

Every child and grown up I know loves cookies, and chocolate chip cookies are always a winner. Here's a quick recipe that children will enjoy making and, more importantly, eating.

MAKES 36 COOKIES

250g softened butter
120g caster sugar
240g soft brown sugar
2 eggs
1 teaspoon vanilla extract
300g plain flour
220g rolled oats
1 teaspoon baking powder
$\frac{1}{4}$ teaspoon salt

100g cocoa powder
350g chocolate chips

In a large bowl, using a hand blender, cream together the butter and sugars until light and fluffy. Gradually beat in the eggs and vanilla. Combine the flour, oats, baking powder, salt and cocoa powder in a separate bowl. Add them to the creamed mixture and mix well, then stir in the chocolate chips.

Shape the mixture into 36 small balls and place them 5cm apart on ungreased baking trays, pressing each ball down with the back of a fork. Bake in an oven preheated to 190°C/Gas Mark 5 for 10–12 minutes, until lightly browned.

SWEET POTATO CUSTARD

Combining sweet potato with banana makes a delicious dessert. Both bananas and sweet potatoes contain natural sugars, so depending on how sweet your tooth is you may prefer not to add the sugar – thus making this dish low in added sugar and fat.

FOR 6

240g sweet potatoes
2 ripe bananas, mashed
250ml evaporated milk
2 eggs
$\frac{1}{2}$ teaspoon salt
50g raisins
1 tablespoon ground cinnamon, plus 1 teaspoon cinnamon mixed with 2 teaspoons sugar for the topping
2 tablespoons soft brown sugar (optional but I tend to add it)

Boil the sweet potatoes in their skins until tender, then peel and place in a bowl. Mash until smooth. Add the mashed bananas and evaporated milk and stir until combined. Add the eggs, salt, raisins, cinnamon and brown sugar, if using. Place in a non-stick baking tin and sprinkle the cinnamon and sugar mixture over the top. Bake in an oven preheated to 160°C/Gas Mark 3 for 35–40 minutes or until the mixture is golden brown and a fork inserted in the centre comes out clean. Serve with cream, custard or ice cream – or even as an accompaniment to a main course. Like I said, we Americans love to mix sweet and savoury.

POUND CAKE

The very first cake to pass my lips was a pound cake. I will not even say who makes the best pound cake in my family because my grandmother, my mother, all of her sisters (except my Aunt BJ) and my great-aunts all still bake a mean pound cake. Pound cakes are so called because originally they contained a pound each of flour, sugar, butter and eggs, making them very rich and buttery tasting. It is important to make sure the butter and eggs are at room temperature as this enables the maximum amount of air to be beaten into the mixture.

Traditionally, pound cakes are baked in a round bundt tin. I still bake all mine in my grandmother's cake tin. She passed it on to my mother, and I begged her to let me bring it to England with me. It has been in the family for over 50 years and has made some of the best cakes in the world.

300g plain flour
$1/2$ teaspoon baking powder
$1/2$ teaspoon bicarbonate of soda
$1/4$ teaspoon salt
250g butter, at room temperature
200g caster sugar
3 large eggs, at room temperature
1 teaspoon vanilla extract
1 teaspoon lemon extract
$1/2$ teaspoon coconut extract (optional)

Butter and flour a 1.2 litre-capacity bundt tin or ring mould (or two 23 x 12cm loaf tins). Sift the flour, baking powder, bicarbonate of soda and salt into a large bowl and set aside.

In a separate bowl, beat the butter until smooth, preferably with an electric mixer. Add the sugar, a little at a time, being sure to mix it in well. Continue beating on a medium-high speed for about 3–5 minutes, until the mixture is light and fluffy. Add the eggs one at a time, beating well after each addition. Add the vanilla, lemon and coconut extract, if using, and beat in well. Fold in the sifted flour mixture. Spoon into the prepared cake tin and place on the middle shelf of an oven preheated to 160°C/Gas Mark 3. Bake for 35–45 minutes, until the cake is golden brown and a skewer inserted in the centre comes out clean.

Remove the cake from the oven and place the tin on a wire rack to cool. After about 20 minutes, turn the cake out on to a plate. You must leave the cake to cool in the tin a little first, as it may collapse if you try to remove it too soon.

The best thing about pound cake is that it can be eaten straight away, stored in foil or in a cake tin for up to a week, or frozen for a special treat in the future. Serve plain, or dusted with icing sugar.

MY GRANDMOTHER, MY MOTHER, ALL OF HER SISTERS (EXCEPT MY AUNT BJ) AND MY GREAT-AUNTS ALL STILL BAKE A MEAN POUND CAKE.

CHOCOLATE BROWNIES

No American child would believe it's dessert time without brownies on the menu. There are many recipes to choose from but for me the simple ones are always the best. I am a firm believer in adding oil to the mix, and making sure the brownies are a little bit cakey and a whole lot fudgy. In the restaurant, whenever a customer is unsure which dessert to order, I always suggest the brownies because I know they never let me down.

MAKES 12 BROWNIES

100g butter
350g granulated sugar
2 eggs
1 teaspoon vanilla extract
150g self-raising flour, sifted
100g cocoa powder
$1/_4$ teaspoon salt
100ml vegetable oil
100g chocolate chips
100g walnuts, chopped (optional)
vanilla ice cream, to serve
chocolate sauce, to serve

Cream the butter and sugar together until light and fluffy, then gradually beat in the eggs and vanilla. Sift in the flour, cocoa powder and salt and fold in thoroughly. Add the oil and chocolate chips and blend well. Stir in the walnuts, if using. I tend to leave the nuts out, as there are so many people with nut allergies now and I want to make sure everyone can enjoy these goodies.

Spread the mixture evenly in a greased 23cm square tin. Bake in an oven preheated to 180°C/Gas Mark 4 for 35 minutes or until done – a skewer or knife inserted in the centre should come out almost clean, with just a couple of crumbs clinging to it. Cool in the tin on a wire rack, then cut into squares and serve. They are great served warm with ice cream and a drizzle of chocolate sauce.

NO AMERICAN CHILD WOULD BELIEVE IT'S DESSERT TIME WITHOUT BROWNIES ON THE MENU.

DAOOD'S APPLE CAKE

My nephew, Daood, came to visit us in England on his summer vacation for the first time when he was nine years old, with his older cousin, Aja, aged eleven. His mother, Cindi, my sister, was convinced that he would be too shy to stay the whole summer but I begged her to let him try. He ran on to the plane without even looking back. My sister shed a tear as she realised her little boy was growing up. Daood, like myself, soon discovered that England was a country he could relate to. He loved English football more than American football. He adored everything about the lifestyle here and to prove it he regularly spent his summers in the UK with me. When I opened the restaurant he would beg to be allowed to help in the kitchen. To everyone's amazement, he was really good in the pastry section. He had a flair for desserts and began to make all sorts of cakes and pies for me, taking great pride in his creations. His favourite, and mine, was apple cake.

After graduating from high school, he came back to England in 2005 and spent the winter with me. He made the decision to return to America to study catering, so that he could come back with qualifications and become my pastry chef. While home for the summer, he set off with friends to view the university of his choice and was involved in a fatal car crash. I happened to be at home for a family celebration of my brother Craig's fiftieth birthday. The whole family was united for the party when I answered the door to two state troopers, who informed me that my nephew had passed away. The entire family was thrown into deep grief as we mourned Daood's death. He was such a bright and happy young man, who left us at the age of just 19. This apple cake is dedicated to Daood.

FOR 10–12

5 eating apples, peeled, cored and diced
150g caster sugar
150g soft brown sugar
125ml vegetable oil
2 eggs, lightly beaten
2 teaspoons vanilla extract
300g plain flour
2 teaspoons bicarbonate of soda
$\frac{1}{2}$ teaspoon salt

Thoroughly mix the apples and sugar together, then stir in the oil, eggs and vanilla. Sift the dry ingredients together and fold them into the apple mixture. Pour the batter into a well-greased 32 x 23cm cake tin and place in an oven preheated to 180°C/Gas Mark 4. Bake for 35–40 minutes, until a skewer inserted in the centre comes out clean. It should have a nice crust on the top. Serve with ice cream or custard.

PINEAPPLE UPSIDE-DOWN CAKE

This used to be a very popular dessert but nowadays you have to search long and hard for it on menus. Not on mine, though – I have always loved it and make sure my customers can get it whenever they visit the restaurant.

FOR 8-10

170g softened butter
150g caster sugar
1 teaspoon vanilla extract
2 eggs
150g self-raising flour
1 teaspoon baking powder
$1/4$ teaspoon salt

For the topping
120g softened butter
200g soft brown sugar
$1/2$ teaspoon ground cinnamon
6 pineapple rings (a 430g tin, with juice)
maraschino cherries

I like to begin with the topping first. Melt the butter in a saucepan and stir in the brown sugar and cinnamon. Once the butter and sugar are combined, add 50ml of the juice from the pineapples and gently simmer over the lowest possible heat for about 5 minutes.

Arrange the pineapple rings in a square or round 23cm cake tin and place a maraschino cherry in the centre of each one. Pour the sweetened sugar syrup over the pineapple and leave to stand while you make the cake mixture.

Cream together the butter and sugar until pale, then add the vanilla. Beat in the eggs, one at a time. Finally, sift in the flour, baking powder and salt and fold in well. Spoon the cake mixture on top of the pineapple and place in an oven preheated to 180°C/Gas Mark 4. Bake for 40 minutes or until a skewer inserted in the centre comes out clean. Allow the cake to cool in the tin for about 20 minutes, then turn out on to a plate, so the pineapple is on top. Serve warm, with ice cream.

SOUTHERN BISCUITS

Let's get one thing straight: when an American wants a biscuit, they are talking about a type of bread and not sweet round things. No siree, we call those cookies. Biscuits have been around for centuries and because they are so easy to make, they are here to stay. They are made with baking powder rather than yeast, rather like an English scone but without the fruit. If we add fruit, then we tend to include extra sugar and raisins and turn them into sweet Cinnamon Buns (page 154). A sweet biscuit topped with fresh fruit is more commonly known as a shortcake. Biscuits don't necessarily need to be rolled out. They can simply be dropped from a spoon, when they are known as drop biscuits.

MAKES ABOUT 16 BISCUITS

450g plain flour
1 tablespoon baking powder
$1/2$ teaspoon salt
135g Trex vegetable fat (solid form for pastry)
140–150ml milk

Sift the flour, baking powder and salt into a bowl. Add the vegetable fat and cut it in with the aid of 2 knives, using them in a scissor action. Stir in enough milk to make a soft dough. Knead lightly on a floured board until smooth, then roll or pat out to about 1cm thick. Using a 5cm pastry cutter or a small teacup, cut out rounds and place on an ungreased baking tray. Bake in an oven preheated to 230°C/Gas Mark 8 for 10–12 minutes, until golden brown.

LET'S GET ONE THING STRAIGHT:
WHEN AN AMERICAN WANTS A BISCUIT,
THEY ARE TALKING ABOUT A TYPE OF
BREAD AND NOT SWEET ROUND THINGS.
NO SIREE, WE CALL THOSE COOKIES.

CINNAMON BUNS

This is a sweet variation on the biscuit recipe on page 152, combining my candied sauce and raisins. They are delicious and can be frozen.

MAKES ABOUT 16 BUNS

450g plain flour
1 tablespoon baking powder
$^1/_2$ teaspoon salt
110g Trex vegetable fat (solid form for pastry)
140–150ml milk
240g softened butter
150g soft brown sugar, plus extra for sprinkling
2 tablespoons ground cinnamon
115g raisins

Sift the flour, baking powder and salt into a bowl. Add the vegetable shortening and cut it in with the aid of 2 knives, using them in a scissor action. Stir in enough milk to make a soft dough. Knead lightly on a floured board until smooth, then roll or pat out into a square about 2.5cm thick.

Melt 200g of the butter in a saucepan, then add the brown sugar and 1 tablespoon of cinnamon. Stir together and, as the mixture thickens, bring it to the boil. Remove from the heat and divide three-quarters of the sauce between two 23cm round cake tins. Set aside.

Spread the remaining butter over the dough. Pour the remaining candied sauce on top and sprinkle with the raisins. Roll up the pastry from both ends to meet in the centre and then separate the 2 rolls. With a sharp knife, cut the rolled-up pastry into slices about 5cm thick and arrange them side by side in the tins. They should look like spiral pinwheels. Sprinkle the remaining cinnamon and a little brown sugar on top and bake in an oven preheated to 230°C/Gas Mark 8 for 15–20 minutes, until golden brown.

INDEX

ACKNOWLEDGEMENTS

There are many, many people that I would like to acknowledge and thank. My journey in writing this book has been filled with good times, some bad times and some down-right stressful times, but through it all, I have received great love and support from my family, friends and more importantly from those special people who didn't even know me, but offered their help and support. I'll start with them, because although my friends and family have been there from the start they weren't able to give me the professional advice and head start that I needed. These people have all been where I am trying to get to. They already have the books, the shows, and, most importantly, the public on their side. So, I salute and thank them first and then I'll move on to my loved ones.

Number one has to be Gordon Ramsay. I joke when I refer to him as my cousin, but those days he spent with me were equivalent to a five year university degree. He taught, I listened and I have tried my best to stick to his advice. He did the best thing he could ever have done – he ate and enjoyed my food, he suggested I put my recipes into a book, he showed me and my team the way, and he made it possible for me and the restaurant to be where we are today. Christine Hall, the producer and director of *Kitchen Nightmares*, who was always honest and supportive. Simon Wright, for helping us during and after the show, and everyone who worked on the programme from Optomen Television. Anthony Worral Thompson and all the professional celebrity chefs I have worked with, for allowing me – a complete unknown – to work alongside them and share my soul food recipes on their shows. I mustn't forget the power of local, national and international TV, radio, the worldwide web and all other media forms, which have featured me and introduced Soul in a Bowl and my struggle to the world. Jon Croft and everyone at Absolute Press,

my publishers, for asking and allowing me to write this book. Peter Cassidy, for his fantastic photography, which makes my food look as delicious as it tastes! Jane Middleton and Trish Hilferty – they both helped me to better understand the metric system (I think I've almost cracked it now!). Jack Tang, former owner of Choys Chinese restaurant and the place that has now become the home of Momma's Big House, Colbert Macalister PR, my agents at MyJam Ltd, Paul Robinson, and all the hard-working businesses of Brighton and Hove, who have offered us a helping hand. These are the people who didn't necessarily know who I was but who have all in their own way helped me keep the faith.

By writing a book I have been allowed to enter into complete strangers' lives and homes and introduce them to the food I grew up on and love so much.

MY AMERICAN FAMILY

It all began with my mother, the Reverend Daisy Thomas and my father Harold Thomas, my brothers Craig and his wife Tanya, Curt and his wife Ada, my sister Cindi and her husband Daood. My nephews Daood and Christopher, my nieces Aja, Ciani, Ari and Akia. My grandmothers and grandfather, all of my aunts and uncles, my Aunt Carolyn, (who taught and inspired me to cook), my Aunt BJ, (who put the love of soul and funk music into my soul), my Great Aunts Delia, 86, and Anna, 90 years old, both who came to England last year, 2006, with my mother aged 73, to offer their love and support and help me decorate and open the new Big House. My best friend Robyn, my many childhood friends and everyone else in my family – too large to mention each of them by name. You all know who you are and your love and support is noted.

MY ENGLISH FAMILY

I must begin with my husband Phil Jones, who has been with me every step of the way. We got married in 2000 and one year later we up-rooted the family and moved to Brighton to open the Soul Food Shack. He has, more than anyone, been through the ups and downs with me. He has held me close and reassured me that a change was soon to come, and with this book it has finally happened. My youngest daughter Krystin, who moved to Brighton with her young son, Tyler, born December 2002, but knew from the first day we opened that working in a restaurant was not the job for her (but that living close to her mum was the perfect way to free baby sitting). My eldest daughter, Katryna, on the other hand, has been by my side and is my rock. She left her job in London to come to our rescue, and took on the role as restaurant manager. She has now rewarded me with a beautiful granddaughter, Ellis Faye, born December 2006, and has joined her sister, ensuring that I have no weekends free. Harvey and Edgar who will always be special to me, Eleanor and all the members of my husband Phil's family, for understanding the pressures associated with running a busy restaurant, which have made it difficult for us to socialize. Ray Shell, my first husband and father to my daughters, who has always encouraged me and been positive and supportive and who understands what it means to be a part of a strong and loving family. As a former foster carer, I must thank all of the social workers and children which were in my care, 'cause they kept me in the kitchen, often cooking three or more different dishes at each mealtime, which prepared me for my journey.

MY EXTENDED FAMILY AND FRIENDS

Sarah, Len, Zara and Roley Ilic, all who have been with me through thick and thin; their love and care has been special. Amanda and Lambros, who invited me to Skiathos, Greece, and gave me my first stab at chefing in their restaurant. Andrea, my friend and make-up artist and her kids; Shandy, who put me up in her house when I first came to Brighton; Perrin, for asking me to open and run a small sandwich shop in central Brighton, the summer before we opened the Soul Food Shack; Soo, my close friend who moved from Chiswick to Brighton at the same time as I did and has always been supportive. Lynn and John; Brian, my first chef, and his family for being patient as we struggled to make things work; all of my past and present staff – there have been over 100 of them; Ruth Price, who has been a rock to us all at The Big House; The Hub 100 club; The Brighton Rotary Club, of which I am a member. My first managers, Sue and Ruth Shane, who both inspired me as strong business women, all my friends in Chiswick and all the children I have taught over the years. All the Street Angels; Andy and Anthony from the Edinburgh Fringe Festival 2006; Bert Williams; Jenni and the Brighton BME community; the Sussex Business Awards for making me their Entrepreneur of the Year 2006/07; Wayne Thompson; Ryan Veal; Sean and his production team at Bite TV; all the solicitors, accountants, professional advisors, all our suppliers and even the VAT office who have been there through thick and thin.

Brian, Beth, Marcus, Catherine, Jo, Jonathan, Michael, and many more loyal and regular customers to the restaurant. All past and present customers, and to all the kind people who don't know us but have written to us wishing us success. I even want to thank all of those people out there who have written to me or posted a note on a website to complain. I have tried to learn from all of my mistakes and hopefully with your comments be able to improve our service to the public.

AND LAST BUT NOT LEAST...

I'd like to acknowledge all of my forefathers and the slaves who endured such hardships and yet who gave birth to this wonderful style of cooking. I'm thankful also for my church upbringing and for having God – without Him in my life, none of this would have been possible.